A Three Dog Life

A Three Dog Life

ABIGAIL THOMAS

Weidenfeld & Nicolson

LONDON

First published in Great Britain in 2007
by Weidenfeld & Nicolson

1 3 5 7 9 10 8 6 4 2

The author is grateful to the following magazines and anthologies for publishing
pieces from *A Three Dog Life*: 'Accident' and 'Home' were published in *O*.
'Comfort' was published in the anthology *Dog is My Co-Pilot*. 'The Magnificent
Frigate Bird' and 'Filling What's Empty' were published in *Tin House*. 'Learning to
Live Alone' was published in *Self*. 'Dog Talk' and 'Carolina's in Heat and I'm Not'
were published in *Bark*. 'How to Banish Melancholy' was published in the
anthology *Woman's Best Friend*. 'Guilt' was published in *Subtropics*. 'Knitting 2002 to
Present' was published in *Swivel*. 'The Past, Present, Future' was published in
Real Simple. 'Moving' was published on mrbellersneighborhood.com.

A CIP catalogue record for this book is available
from the British Library

ISBN 978 0 297 85284 1

Printed in Great Britain by Mackays of Chatham plc, Chatham, Kent

Weidenfeld & Nicolson
An imprint of the Orion Publishing Group
Orion House, 5 Upper St Martin's Lane, London WC2H 9EA

The Orion Publishing Group's policy is to use papers that are natural, renewable
and recyclable products and made from wood grown in sustainable forests. The
logging and manufacturing processes are expected to conform to the
environmental regulations of the country of origin.

www.orionbooks.co.uk

For Sally

Australian Aborigines slept with
their dogs for warmth on cold nights,
the coldest being a "three dog night."

—Wikipedia

Thank you to Agnes Wilkie and Jill Aguanno
for insight and wisdom and compassion and
for making me laugh;

and thank you Chuck Verrill, best friend,
for getting it, always, whatever it is.

I

What Stays the Same

THIS IS THE ONE THING THAT STAYS THE same: my husband got hurt. Everything else changes. A grandson needs me and then he doesn't. My children are close then one drifts away. I smoke and don't smoke; I knit ponchos, then hats, shawls, hats again, stop knitting, start up again. The clock ticks, the seasons shift, the night sky rearranges itself, but my husband remains constant, his injuries are permanent. He grounds me. Rich is where I shine. I can count on myself with him.

I live in a cozy house with pretty furniture. Time passes here. There is a fireplace and two acres and the dogs run around and dig big holes and I don't care. I have a twenty-seven-inch TV and lots of movies. The telephone rings often. Rich is lodged in a single moment and it never tips into the next. Last week I lay on his bed in the nursing home and watched him. I was out of his field of vision and I think he forgot I was there. He stood still, then he picked up a newspaper from a neat pile of newspapers, held it a moment, and carefully put it back. His arms dropped to his sides. He looked as if he was waiting for the next thing but there is no next thing.

I got stuck with the past and future. That's my half of this bad hand. I know what happened and I never get used to it. Just when I think I've metabolized everything I am drawn up short. "Rich lost part of his vision" is what I say, but recently Sally told the nurse, "He is blind in his right eye," and I was catapulted out of the safety of the past tense into the now.

TODAY I DRIVE TO THE WOOL STORE. I ARRIVE with my notebook open and a pen.

"What are you doing?" Paul asks.

"I'm taking a poll," I say. "What is the one thing that stays stable in your life?"

"James," says Paul instantly.

"And I suppose James will say Paul," I say, writing down *James*.

"No, he'll say the dogs," says Paul, laughing.

"Creativity," says Heidi, the genius.

"I have to think," says a woman I don't know.

"The dogs," says James.

RICH AND I HAD A HOUSE TOGETHER ONCE. HE was the real gardener. He raked and dug, planted and weeded, stood over his garden proudly. Decorative grasses were his specialty. He cut down my delphiniums when he planted his fountain grass. "Didn't you see them?" I asked. "They were so tall and beautiful." But he was too busy digging to listen. I lost interest in flowers. We planted a hydrangea tree outside the kitchen window. We cut down (after much deliberation) two big prickly bushes that were growing together like eyebrows at either side of our small path. We waited until the birds were done with their young, then Rich planted two more hydrangea trees where the bushes had stood. I don't want to see how big they are by now, how beautiful their heavy white blossoms look when it rains. "I love what you've done with the garden," my friend Claudette says, looking at the bed of overgrown nettles in my backyard. I weeded there exactly once. I want to plant fountain grass out there, but first I need a backhoe.

RICH AND I DON'T HAVE THE NORMAL UPS AND downs of a marriage. I don't get impatient. He doesn't have to figure out what to do with his retirement. I don't watch him go through holidays with the sorrow of missing his absent children. Last week we were walking down the hall to his room, it was November, we had spent the afternoon together. "If I wasn't with you and we weren't getting food, the dark would envelop my soul," he said cheerfully.

He never knows I'm leaving until I go.

II

Accident

M Y HUSBAND AND I MET TWELVE YEARS ago after he answered a personal ad I placed in the *New York Review of Books*. We met at the Moon Palace restaurant on Broadway and 112th Street. It was raining, he carried a big umbrella. He had beef with scallions and I had sliced sautéed fish. It took me about five minutes to realize this was the nicest man in the world and when he asked me to marry him thirteen days later I said yes. He was fifty-seven, I was forty-six. Why wait? We still have the magazine. I used to look at the page full of ads, mine the only one he'd circled, and feel the fragility of our luck. "Thank you for the happiest year of my life," he wrote on our first anniversary. We envisioned an old age on a front porch somewhere, each other's comfort, companions for life. But life takes twists and turns. There is good luck and bad.

Yesterday in his hospital room my husband asked urgently, "Will you move me twenty-six thousand miles to the left?" "Yes," I said, not moving from my chair. After a moment he said, "Thank you," adding in wonder, "I didn't feel a thing." "You're welcome," I answered. "Are we alone?" he asked. "We are," I answered, the nurse's aide having stepped out for a moment. "What happened to Stacy and the flounder?" he said, and I saw the hospital room as he must experience it, a kind of primordial twilight soup, an atmosphere in which a flounder might well be swimming through midair. The image stays with me.

My husband is having brain surgery next week. Today I am sitting in the dog park. The weather is what Rich would call "a soft day." This is the place I try to make sense of things, order them, to tame what happened. Our beagle, Harry, makes his way around the perimeter of the dog run, with his nose to the ground. He is a loner. I, too, sit by myself, but I pay attention to everything. "Suffering is the finest teacher," said an old friend long ago. "It teaches you details." I didn't know what he was talking about. I do now. I watch the dogs, one tiny dachshund so skinny he looks like a single stroke of calligraphy. An elderly man with a very young chow reaches down to pat my dog. Harry skips away.

"Very good," answers another man, who has just been asked how he is. It has been a long time since I answered that question that way.

Monday, April 24, at nine forty at night, our doorman Pedro called me on the intercom. "Your dog is in the elevator," he said. The world had just changed forever, and I think I knew it even then. "My dog? Where is my husband?" I asked. "I don't know. But your dog is in the elevator with 14E. You'd better go get him." I stepped into the hall in my bathrobe. The elevator door opened and a neighbor delivered Harry to me. "Where is my husband?" I asked again, but my neighbor didn't know. Harry was trembling. Rich must be frantic, I thought. Then the buzzer rang again. "Your husband has been hit by a car," Pedro said, "113th and Riverside. Hurry."

Impossible, impossible. Where were my shoes? My skirt? I was in slow motion, moving underwater. I looked under the bed, found my left shoe, grabbed a sweater off the back of a chair. This couldn't be serious. I threw my clothes on and got into the elevator. Then I ran along Riverside and when I saw the people on the sidewalk ahead I began to run faster, calling his name. What kind of injury drew such a crowd?

I found my husband lying in a pool of blood, his head split open. Red lights were flashing from cop cars and emergency vehicles and the EMS people were kneeling over his body. "Let them work," said a police officer, as I tried to fight my way next to him, managing to get close enough to touch his hand. They were cutting the clothes off him, his Windbreaker, his flannel shirt. Somebody pulled me away. "Don't look," he said, but I needed to look, I needed to keep my eyes on him. A policeman began asking me questions. "You're his wife? What's his name? Date of birth? What's your name? Address?" Then as I watched they loaded Rich onto a stretcher and into the ambulance. I wanted to climb in too but they sped off without me. A policeman drove me to the emergency room at St. Luke's Hospital, three blocks away. The superintendent of our building, Cranston Scott, came with me, stayed until my family arrived, gave me his credit card number to call my children and my sisters. I called Rich's former wife, who had the numbers of Rich's children, his brother, Gil. I waited in a small room outside the emergency room at the hospital while dozens of hospital personnel went through the door where my husband lay. I found out later that the accident report the police filled out listed Rich as "dead, or likely to die."

Harry wanders over. He looks up at me and I reach down to stroke his head, his ears. He comes to me to reassure himself that I am still there, I think, or perhaps to reassure me that he is still there. He was a stray; we adopted him from a friend into whose yard he had wandered, starved and terrified, a year ago. Rich hadn't wanted a dog. Every time I dragged him to look at yet another puppy I'd discovered in yet another pet store, he would look at it and say something like "Yes, but isn't his face a bit rodentlike?" When I took him to met Harry he said, "Well, that's a very nice little dog." Five months later Harry got off his leash and Rich ran into Riverside Drive to save him. I don't look at Harry and think, If only we hadn't got him. I don't blame myself for this accident, or our dog, although I believe if it had been a child who was hurt I probably would. We were two adults living our lives and this terrible thing happened. I don't find it ironic that the very reason Rich got hurt is the creature who comforts me. There is no irony here, no room for guilt or second-guessing. That would be a diversion, and indulgence. These are hard facts to be faced head-on. We are in this together, my husband and I, we have been thrown into this unfamiliar country with different weather, different rules. Everything I think and do matters now, in a way it never has before.

I seem to be leaving in the road behind me all sorts of unnecessary baggage, stuff too heavy to carry. Old fears are evaporating, the claustrophobia that crippled me for years is gone, vanished. I used to climb the thirteen flights to our apartment because I was terrified of being alone in the elevator. What if it got stuck? What if I never got out? Then there I was one Sunday morning in the hospital, Rich on the eighth floor, the elevator empty. What had for years terrified me now seemed ridiculously easy. I haven't got the time for this, I thought, and got right in. When the doors closed I kept thinking, Go ahead! Try it! What more can you possibly do to me?

The head injury my husband sustains is a traumatic brain injury, specifically damage to the frontal lobes; part of his brain descended into his sinus cavities, dragging arteries along with it. There is a hole or holes in his dura, the casing around the brain; his skull is fractured like a spiderweb. Everywhere. The danger of meningitis is real. They must remove the dead brain tissue, repair the dura, relieve the pressure in the buildup of fluid, repair the damage to his skull. It is a long surgery, and carries with it its own danger of infection. The surgery was scheduled three weeks ago but had to be postponed when Rich developed a fever three days before.

He was fine in the morning, and in a good mood, but by afternoon he felt warm to my touch, and he was unlike himself, unlike any version of himself. He spoke in a low raspy voice like Jimmy Cagney, and I couldn't reel him back from the deep water he seemed to be in. I knew that one of the early signs of meningitis is a personality change and I was scared. The doctors immediately treated him as if this were meningitis, and bags of sinister yellow liquids dripped into his arm. The lumbar puncture came back negative, but the surgery was postponed until his fever went down.

It is June, the weather is warm, and Harry is shedding. When I brush him he stands absolutely still. At night he sleeps in bed with me. I feel his warm breath on my neck, his ear "like a velvet lily pad," as Rich described it, against my cheek. I don't sleep on Rich's side of the bed, Rich's side is Rich's side, his pajamas still neatly tucked under his pillow. When I first saw them, and his trousers over the back of the chair, I wept. When I think about the past I get sad, our mornings of coffee and the newspaper. After his shower he would appear in the kitchen with the bathroom wastebasket in his hands, announcing "the naked dustman." I miss my husband. I miss the comfort of living with this man I loved and trusted absolutely. When I gave a reading in May, I missed his shining face among the others. I missed his pride in me, his impulse to take everyone in the audience out for dinner. Walking down our street I missed him by my side. The past gets swallowed up in the extraordinary circumstances of now. But mostly it hurts too much to let my mind go back.

My son called last night. "Are you worried about the operation?" he asked. "I don't think so," I answered. It is what I have heard one of the surgeons call "meat and potatoes" surgery. What terrifies me is seeing Rich in the recovery room. This doesn't make any sense, but I keep remembering his face just after his accident, ruined beyond recognition, blood pooling in the corners of his swollen eyes. Those first days his daughter, Sally, and I took twelve-hour shifts at the hospital, sitting in a chair next to his bed, listening to the beeping of monitors in the ICU. We were afraid to leave him. It was as if we were trying to hatch an egg, keeping him warm with our presence, and we didn't want him to wake without a familiar face nearby. *"¿Qué pasa?"* were the first words he spoke when the doctors removed his breathing tube. I put my ear close to his mouth. *"¿Qué pasa?"* This man who failed Spanish. It is a funny miracle.

I am sitting on my bench; behind me three dogs are digging a hole to China. The odd woman who wears a Band-Aid across her nose and white gloves, who often stands at the gate excoriating dogs and their owners with tales of being trailed by the FBI, has just sat down next to me. She has a whippet. Whippets, she tells me, were dogs that hunted rats in the mines. "Wales, or Scotland or Ireland," she goes on. There being no room to break their necks in the small spaces, they twirled and twirled, snapping the rat's necks that way. "That's interesting," I say cautiously. Talk moves on and about, like a dog looking for a good place to lie down. Somehow we speak of the old radio shows. Clyde Beatty, *Sky King*, *Sergeant Preston of the Yukon*. She asks do I remember the real-estate offering they made? I shake my head. "You could buy one inch in Alaska," she says. All day I can't get the idea of owning an inch of the Alaskan wilderness out of my head. I am searching for meaning in everything.

In the first weeks after his accident, Rich spoke in mysteries. It was as if he were now connected to some vast reservoir of wisdom, available only to those whose brains have been altered, a reservoir unencumbered by personality, quirks, history, habits. "It is interesting to think that one could run farther and longer and perhaps find the answer," he said one evening, drifting in and out of delirious talk. "What would you get to?" I asked, eager for the answer. "The allure of distance" was what he said, a dreamy phrase.

Last week, as he struggled to make sense of the world, unable to find words, my youngest daughter, Catherine, came to visit. "Do you know who I am?" she asked, and he peered at her intently. "Do you eat field mice?" he asked, a strange question we thought, until I realized the first three letters of her name spell "cat." Perhaps this was a glimpse of how the mind pieces things together after an assault, trying to rewire itself. "The goat's mouth is full of stones," he said one day, and I leave that as it is, a mystery. During the days when it is impossible to communicate in words, I get into his bed and we hold hands. Nap therapy. This is a familiar posture, something we can do without speech, without thinking.

How are you managing? friends ask. How are you doing this? They leave me food and flowers, they send me letters and messages. They pray. I love these people, I love my family. Doing what? I wonder. This is the path our lives have taken. A month ago I would have thought this life impossible. Sometimes I feel as if I'm trying to rescue a drowning man, and I only have time to rise to the surface for one gasp of air before I go back down again. There is an exhilaration to it, a high born only partly of exhaustion, and I find myself almost frighteningly alive. There is nothing like calamity for refreshing the moment. Ironically, the last several years my life had begun to feel shapeless, like underwear with the elastic gone, the days down around my ankles. Now there is an intensity to the humblest things—buying paper towels, laundry detergent, dog food, keeping the household running in Rich's absence. One morning I buy myself a necklace made of sea glass, and it becomes a talisman. Shopping contains the future. As my daughter Jennifer says, shopping is hope.

On the day of Rich's surgery, his daughter, Sally, and I are there at six thirty in the morning to accompany him to the operating room. We walk beside the stretcher and try to calm him, but he is disoriented and very agitated, until the anesthesiologist gives him an injection of Versed. "Can we get some of that to go?" asks Sally. When they wheel him into the operating theater we go to have breakfast in the hospital cafeteria. Sally has two boiled eggs, Cream of Wheat, corned beef hash, and coffee; she's a nurse and she knows what she's doing, it's going to be a long day. I have a banana. The waiting room is a large place with high ceilings, and through a sliver of window I can see the brightly colored clothes of pint-sized campers out on Fifth Avenue with their nannies, the green of Central Park behind them. Outside the weather is cool and clear, and Sally and I settle down for the long wait. The surgery is expected to take all day. I am not worried about Rich, but my dog has gotten sick, his ears were hot and he didn't eat, his stool was bloody. My sister Judy has agreed to take him to the vet. Suddenly panicky, I begin calling my sister every fifteen minutes. Patiently her son tells me his mother is still at the vet. I can't think straight, what would I do without Harry? Finally in my desperation I call the vet himself. It turns out Harry has colitis and all I need to do is feed him lots of rice and give him medicine for five days. This is such a huge relief that I wonder for a second why I was so worried and then it hits me that I comfort Rich, but Harry comforts me.

At six o'clock we find out that Rich's surgery has gone well. We can go up and see him in the recovery room, the SICU. He is asleep, bandages around his head, beneath them are the staples that cross his head from ear to ear. The doctors have done what they set out to do. There being no bone left unsplintered in his forehead (shattered like an eggshell, they tell us), they have built him a new one, made of titanium. They have rebuilt the floor of his brain, they have removed the dead tissue. The brain fluid that had been building up is relieved. His right frontal lobe is gone, and the left damaged. They tell us again that there will be differences in Rich's personality, only time will tell the nature of the changes. I have never processed this information. Changes? Just give him back to me and everything will be all right. We begin the round of phone calls to friends and family.

But in the days immediately following the surgery Rich enters the stage known as "Inappropriate Behavior." This is euphemistic for the anger and irrationality that is part of the process of recovery. Rich is angry and confused. He doesn't mention going home; there is no destination except "out of here." I betray him all the time, he says, by not saving him. He thought he could trust me, he thought we loved each other, but now our love seems very thin to him, he says. Roughly he pushes my hand away as I reach for his. My feelings are hurt, I can't help it, although I try to reason them away. Sitting with him hour after hour, his face glowering, makes me think of the stories I've heard of people who after traumatic brain injury bore no resemblance to their former selves. I am terrified that a change like this will undo me. This man is not the man I married. None of this is his doing, he didn't choose this, but neither did I.

One day I look out the hospital window high above Central Park, and I feel as if there's a tightrope connecting Rich's hospital room to our apartment, and all I do is walk back and forth on it, the city far below. I can almost see it shivering like a high-tension wire above the trees. This is when I learn that I have to take care of myself, even if my leaving makes him angry, or worse, sad. I need to eat and sleep. I need to do something mindless, go to a movie, fritter away an afternoon. And I realize something even more startling: I can't make everything all right. It's his body that is hurt, not mine. I can't fix it, I can't make it never have happened.

Rich still refuses food and medicine, everything has been poisoned. "Why are you so fatuous?" he asks angrily as I try to say something cheery about the potassium in a banana. Remarks like this sting me, especially because I sound like Pollyanna even to myself. When we wheel him down a hospital hall for a CAT scan, he says, "You always know you're in for it when you're going down a long hall with nobody else in it."

Afterward he tells me, "I felt I was at a casual execution." When he's lost almost thirty pounds they put a peg in his stomach. Through this tube, which resembles a monkey's tail as it curls out from under the covers to the IV pole, they give him nourishment and medicine. The shape of the tube may be what gives rise to Rich's belief that there is literally a monkey in the bed. "There's no monkey," I tell him. "Don't be so sure," he says, lifting the sheet to peer beneath it.

How do I separate the old Rich from this new Rich, what allowances do I make for his injury, when do I draw the line? How do I draw the line? The nurses say this is just a stage but I am not comforted. I miss my old husband. I miss the old me. When I run across something from before the accident, a snapshot of Rich smiling his beautiful smile, I feel such staggering loss. What happened? Where did my husband go? I clean the closet and find a tiny portable fan Rich bought me for trips because I can't sleep without white noise, and it makes me cry.

"I DON'T KNOW WHO I AM," RICH SAYS OVER AND over. "There are too many thoughts inside my head. I am not myself." Yesterday he said, "Pretend you are walking up the street with your friend. You are looking in windows. But right behind you is a man with a huge roller filled with white paint and he is painting over everywhere you've been, erasing everything. He erases your friend. You don't even remember his name." The image makes me shiver, but he seems exultant in his description. There are days when he is grounded in the here and now and days when his brain is boiling over with confusion. When he is angry I go home after only a short visit. Staying does neither of us any good. Where do I put these bad days? Part of me is still hanging on to the couple we were. Where do I put my anger? What right have I to be angry? My husband is hurt. Part of him is destroyed. I don't even feel my anger most of the time, but it's there, and I only acknowledge it when I find myself doing something self-destructive, going for a day or two without eating, drinking too much coffee, allowing myself to get lonely, tired.

"Good things happen slowly," said a doctor in the ICU months ago, "and bad things happen fast." Those were comforting words, and they comfort me today. Recovery is a long, slow process. There are good days and bad days for both of us. I try to find an even keel but still I am upset on the bad days and hopeful on the good. Uncertainty is the hardest part. There is no prognosis, no one can tell me how much better Rich will get and how long it might take. The day before my birthday Rich imagines that we've gone to Coney Island and he bought me a shell necklace. This is my present, as real for me as it was for him. He held my hand. That was yesterday, a good day, but filled with sadness. The season is changing, I take Harry to the park and watch the leaves turning and falling, there is beauty overhead and underfoot. There is something else I don't know yet, something I'm straining to feel, as subtle as the change in humidity or temperature, or the shift in light as summer becomes fall, the most beautiful season, with its gift of beauty in loss, and the promise of something more to come.

Always when I ride out to Manhasset the train passes through Flushing, where my father grew up. I remember a clapboard house, hydrangea bushes. I remember his father's office to the left when you came in, a long leather couch, glass cases of medical instruments. I remember a mysterious interior, a room to the right, carpeting with a pattern of faded flowers, a carpet that turns up now and again in stories I never finish. I remember bathtubs with iron ball-and-claw feet, a gas fire, a kitchen with (I think) a cream and green enamel stove at which my grandma made three different kinds of meat for Thanksgiving. She also beat an egg into a small glass of sherry for my grandfather to drink every day, a ritual we children were fascinated to watch. In the backyard was an oak planted when my father was born, and over a cement wall in the way back was the Long Island Rail Road. I know the house disappeared years and years ago, but I want to find the bit of wall we peered over, and down what was probably not so steep and long an embankment as I recall, to watch the passing trains. I stare out the window every time we go through Flushing. Long gone the radiators that my grandma banged on every morning to wake her five children. Long gone the smell of baking bacon. Long gone and dispersed that family. But I remember the smell of the gas fire, the stairs that led to the second and third floors. The slate

opening and closing the drawers in his small dresser. "I'm looking for a blanket to cover you with," he says.

Tonight home is another restaurant in my neighborhood, as familiar as grass, little candles burning on every table, lots of people leaning toward each other, talking their heads off. I like this. I sit by myself at the window. I know every inch of the sidewalk, all the stores—it's where I want my ashes scattered after all— starting here at 112th Street down to H&H Bagels on 81st and Broadway. Across the street I can see the pale blue and purple neon of the Deluxe Diner, the yellow lights of Pertutti's, where my husband and I used to eat several times a week. On the corner is Tom's, bad food but famous because of *Seinfeld.* It's getting to be spring. I order another Manhattan although I am already where I want to be, in that dappled place that precedes inebriation. When I go home I will look at the bookcases my husband and I bought thirteen years ago and remember with what relish he tore down the homemade shelves installed by an old boyfriend (a hundred nails in every foot of wood). He painted the bathroom a pale pink, canceling the crazy electric blue someone else had made it years ago. He was making his mark, erasing traces of other periods in my life, the outward and visible manifestations that troubled him and worried his aesthetic. Under his happy and relieved gaze I threw out my deep plush armchairs, one purple, the other a deep royal blue. Their springs were sprung and their arms were balding but they reminded me of the lobbies of old movie theaters with names like the Bijou or the Roxy. Together we bought a couch from Altman's; we re-covered two chairs he had brought with him in a sober dark green fabric. Respectability. We hung my husband's bird prints and I made him put up his running trophies. When periodically I went through closets and threw things away wholesale, he joked that if he weren't careful he'd be on the dustheap too. At first this made me laugh, later I was indignant. Who did he think I was? Didn't he know he was my husband? My companion for life? I don't throw human beings away, I said huffily.

By now, ten o'clock, I'm on my second Manhattan. Rich has forgotten I was there at all today. He thinks we have missed the train to Providence and is very upset. I can't imagine what this form of hell must feel like. The trivial analogy I make to myself is the time I lost my pocketbook at the Minneapolis airport. After the initial shock, and the immediate dilemma caused by not having my airline tickets, identification, or money, I found what I missed most was not the credit cards or driver's license, not the cell phone or cash, not even my lipstick. What I missed was my chum over my shoulder, the reassurance of rummaging through the whole mess, my fingers closing on my jumble of keys, the odd Kleenex, an old cigarette pack with one bent cigarette inside, through the little bits and pieces of detritus, proof I'd been living my life. Here's the ticket stub, here's the receipt from my framer, here is the checkbook with no checks left but a note scribbled to myself on the back, here are my real checks. Without my bag, I had no comfort, no sense of being at home with myself, a chunk of me had gone missing. This is what my husband has lost. The everyday memories of what he had for breakfast, that day follows night, the jingle of loose coins in his pocket. He has no short-term memory. He must invent it for himself.

Twenty years ago I asked a friend if he felt (as I did) a kind of chronic longing, a longing I wanted to identify. "Of course," he answered. We were having lunch by the pond at 59th Street, watching the ducks. The sun was out, the grass was thick and green, the ducks paddled around in the not very blue pond. I was between lives. "What is it?" I asked. "What is it we are longing for?" He thought a minute and said, "There isn't any it. There is just the longing for it." This sounded exactly right. Years later and a little wiser, I know what the longing was for: *here is where I belong.*

Last August, after three months in two hospitals, Rich returned to our apartment. He seemed to be him-

had changed. I don't know. As the days went by he got angrier. Why had I done this? Why was I trying to trick him? Why was I lying? His "real" home was upstairs, or downstairs, anywhere but where he was. Then one morning Rich woke up believing that he had an eleven o'clock appointment with the Gestapo. He was afraid, but resigned. "There is no Gestapo," I said over and over, my arms around his shoulder. "We are safe, you are having a bad dream." But he was convinced otherwise.

His delusions multiplied, there were strangers in his room at night. There were animals running loose. His urine was contaminated, he had sent it to Atlanta, where was the number of the NIH? He had to call them immediately. Soon my own idea of normal began to erode. The floor was tilted under his feet and I began to adjust my gait to his. Home was now a place of chaos and fear. Repeated calls to his doctor were not helpful, and Rich sank further into a paranoid existence that finally became a full-blown psychosis. One night he got out of the apartment at five A.M., barefoot, dressed only in his underwear. "Don't try and stop me," he yelled. "I'm going home." The nurse who came every night drew me aside. "Mrs. Rogin," she said to me, "in this household the insane are ruling the sane." Until that moment, I had been lost in the vortex. We finally found a doctor to treat him, and a hospital that was prepared to admit him through the ER, but though terrified and confused and furious, he wouldn't go. One awful Wednesday morning he insisted again on going home. I brought him his wheelchair. "Get in, Rich," I said, hating myself, "get in. I'll take you home."

THIS IS A BIG MANHATTAN, BUT IT'S MY THIRD AND I allow myself three. Three keeps me from having four. I hadn't had a drink in twenty years before Rich's injury. But in the past year I have returned to drinking and smoking. I drink my drink, I light a cigarette. Familiar ways, the old ways of coping with stress, part of who I was for forty years, not the best part. When I drank my first Manhattan it tasted like home. I told Rich tonight that I loved him. He said, "That's worth twenty hats and all the signatures in the world." I take another swallow. I don't know if my husband will ever be home again. Anywhere.

My friend at the duck pond now owns a stone house in the green hills somewhere in Massachusetts. He doesn't go there often, he lives in New York City. He thinks he should probably sell it to someone who will live there all the time, love it and care for it. But he says every time he gets there, for the first five minutes he knows he is exactly where he belongs. He is at home. Then, restless inside his own skin, he loses the feeling.

But those five minutes every month or so make it worth hanging on to.

I finish my third drink, pay my bill, and walk a straight line down the long block home. Our apartment is filled with my husband and with his absence. Tonight, fueled by sadness, anger, and three drinks, I manage to move the ten-foot-long table it took three men to get into the study, out of the study. It is a table my father used to write on, very old, a trestle table that weighs — I don't know what it weighs, only that in the morning I can't even lift it. But tonight I get it through the door, down the hall, and in front of the bookcases in six minutes from start to finish. Tonight I need to change something. On the table I place the little copper church Rich gave me the third time we met. There are bells in its steeple. I remember thanking him and thinking, Is this some kind of proposal? It was. Thirteen years ago.

Tonight is a hard night. So many broken pieces of our life to try and fit into my sense of past and future, but I am lucky—I know what has changed, I know where I am. Rich's compass is gone, he has no direction home. Nothing is as real to him as the ghost of his memory. But we're all looking for the place we belong. And what is home, anyway, but what we cobble together out of our changing selves? Maybe there isn't any it, as my friend said, only the longing.

Comfort

EVERY OCTOBER THE CATHEDRAL OF SAINT John the Divine celebrates the Feast of Saint Francis and is host to a ceremony known as the Blessing of the Animals. Thousands of people come with their pets, the enormous church is crowded to overflowing. A farm provides some of the bigger beasts, the humble cows and horses and sheep who make a procession to the altar, their necks garlanded with flowers. There are snakes and giant parrots and eagles and hawks. Once there was even an elephant. Outside in the parking lot are small petting zoos; a litter of piglets was especially popular. The peacocks who live on the grounds of the cathedral strut their stuff. The year I went, 2001, the brave dogs who searched the burning graveyard that had been the World Trade Center were honored along with their human companions. A lot of us couldn't stop crying.

I spotted Rosie from half a block away; she was sitting under a table in the parking lot with two other dogs up for adoption. It really was love at first sight, although she looked like a handful—high-strung, and nervous. Half-dachshund, half-whippet (a union that must have come with an instruction sheet), she was simply the most beautiful creature I'd ever seen. She looked like a miniature deer, a gazelle, or a dachshund's dream come true, as someone remarked, looking at Rosie's long legs. Is she housebroken? Spayed? I asked a few unnecessary questions. I knew I wanted her no matter what. I knelt down and stroked her silky brown coat, and looked into a very nervous pair of brown eyes. Her slender body quivered. I had been thinking about a second dog, and here she was.

My beagle, Harry, didn't exactly jump for joy when Rosie arrived. In fact he growled. He was occupying his half of the sofa (which he takes in the middle) and Rosie's approach was unwelcome, to say the least. But he looked a little more alive, I was happy to see. Harry and I had both been leading a reclusive life for a long time, neither of us inclined to leave the house unless we had to. Since the accident Harry had refused to go out. I had to carry him trembling into the elevator, through the lobby, across the street into Riverside Park, and once I put him down he lunged toward home. I had taken his photograph with me to church that day, he would not have liked being there.

Harry had been with us only four months when the accident happened. We had gotten him through a friend who'd found him starving in the woods. The day he arrived we were worried: we gave him food but he wouldn't eat; we put down water but he wouldn't drink; we took him for walks and he skulked close to the ground, his tail between his legs. If we approached him, he tried to make himself as small as possible in a corner of the sofa. Finally, despairing, we went to bed. Ten minutes later we heard the click of toenails across the bare floor and then there was Harry, in bed with us. It was going to be all right. It was going to be better than all right.

"How do you feel about your dog now?" I recall someone asking soon after the disaster. "I love my dog," I said. It seemed a peculiar question. "I couldn't get through this without Harry." In the first weeks of Rich's hospitalization I would often wake in the night to reach for him only to find that the warmth I felt at my side was Harry's small body. In those moments grief and gratitude combined in a way I have since gotten accustomed to.

After some initial squabbling over property rights, Harry and Rosie reached a détente. The only real fight they had was over a glazed doughnut I had foolishly left within reach, but it was an Entenmann's doughnut, well worth fighting for. Within days of Rosie's arrival Harry was out and about, his tail held high. Now we head off for the dog run every morning. Walking Rosie is like having a kite on the end of a leash while Harry stumps along maturely, a small solid anchor. In the dog run Harry and I sit on the bench watching as Rosie runs, leaps, bounds, races any dog who will follow her and outruns all of them except two — a saluki named Sophie and an Afghan named Chelsea. They are the only dogs faster than Rosie but most days they are too elegant to run at all.

Rosie got us out of our slump, but she sleeps with one eye open, if I so much as sigh she is alert. If I look up from my book, or take off my reading glasses, she is tensed to follow. I found out that her owner died in the World Trade Center, and she had been brought to the shelter by a weeping relative. Whoever the man was, he must have loved her as I do, he trained her, and when I tell her to sit and she sits, I swear I can feel his ghost hovering nearby. I want to tell the people who loved him that his dog is part of a family now, that she is doing fine.

I visit my husband once a week. Now he is cared for in a facility upstate that specializes in traumatic brain injury. The accident was more than two years ago, and I still can't get my mind around it. He is there and not there, he is my husband and not my husband. His thoughts seem to break apart and collide with each other, and I try not to think at all. On good days we sit outside. We don't talk, we just sit very close together and hold hands. It feels like the old days, it feels like being married again. When I get home at night my dogs greet me, Rosie bounding as if on springs, Harry wiggling at my feet. Sometimes I sit right down on the floor before taking off my coat.

If you were to look into our apartment in the late morning, or early afternoon, or toward suppertime, you might find us together sleeping. Of course a good rainy day is preferable, but even on sunny summer days, the dogs and I get into bed. Rosie dives under the quilt on my right, Harry on my left, and we jam ourselves together. After a little bit Harry starts to snore, Rosie rests her chin on my ankle, the blanket rises and falls with our breathing, and I feel only gratitude. We are doing something as necessary to our well-being as food or air or water. We are steeping ourselves, reassuring ourselves, renewing ourselves, three creatures of two species, finding comfort in the simple exchange of body warmth.

I'd assumed a puppy but eleven years old (what do you feed her—I want to eat that) leapt to assist me, but I hadn't broken anything. The jitters came from not wearing the full complement of underwear de rigueur for a woman my age but it was so hot, and I just hadn't bothered, and since this was the way I wandered around in the 1960s, maybe I was taken back to those foolish and wild days of fled youth, which I have no desire to revisit.

The nice men and I finished talking about our dogs and as I proceeded into the park I spotted something peculiar in the thickety growth of a young tree. I extricated and examined what turned out to be a four-foot trident, wound round with red and green ribbon, and at the base, a Fuji apple sticker. I glanced around, perhaps the anonymous artist was waiting for his anonymous audience, but there was nobody anywhere. Rosie, who had been pointing, was ready to make her move and Harry was tugging stolidly in the opposite direction so I put the trident back and began to make my gingerly way downhill, acorns scattered like ball bearings all over the place. I stopped once to remove the chicken bone from Harry's mouth and again to comfort Rosie for not being allowed to actually catch the squirrel when every molecule in her quivering body was telling her how. On level ground the three of us were off again, Rosie hunting, Harry sniffing, and me looking for more things people have made.

There is an artist in Riverside Park, maybe a whole bunch of artists. Months ago I found a bunch of smooth round stones, like a clutch of eggs, tucked into the hollow at the base of a tree. Then there was a tiny place setting: knife, fork, spoon, all made of twigs—at the foot of a giant elm. On various tree stumps I've seen arrangements of stones and branches, like offerings on a makeshift altar. Leaning up against a tree near the huge boulder was a complex structure that formed either an unfinished shelter or half a spiderweb made of sticks. I marveled at it for some time, as it seemed to defy the laws of physics, and I wanted to take its picture but by the next morning it had been knocked down. This depressed me until I thought maybe it was the artist himself, dissatisfied with the way things were going. Yesterday a couple of feet off the path in the Bird Sanctuary were two sticks pushed into the ground about four inches apart, and balanced on top was a wavy twig. It made exactly the symbol for pi. Well, this is Columbia territory after all.

I keep an eye out for such things, although I don't talk about it much, aware of my reputation as an enthusiast. "Jennifer!" I exclaimed this summer in Scotland, pointing to a lovely bit of crimson in the grass ahead.

"That's a Kit Kat wrapper, Mom," she said patiently.
And I don't want to sound like a lunatic. I once knew a
woman who told me her house was haunted by a child
who fashioned dolls out of string and lint and rags, and
left them on the stairs for her to find. My hair stood on
end. Thirty years later my hair still stands on end, except now I'm afraid she made the dolls herself. One
evening last week after a heavy rain I saw a lump of
material under a bush by the statue of Louis Kossuth
at 113th Street. This turned out to be a shawl and on
closer inspection to be my own shawl. It must have
fallen from my shoulders one wet windy night and been
blown into the bushes, and now sodden and muddy and
half hidden, it looked like nothing so much as a clue
from a crime scene.

You never know what you'll see. People have been
sleeping in the park these past hot days, one of them a
young man in a red-checked shirt who came into the
dog run because he missed his own dog. He liked my
beagle, Harry. It seems he had had his wallet stolen the
day before and needed his bank card back, but he
didn't want to talk about that, he wanted to talk about
dogs. We chatted for a while; he was soft-spoken. The
next day I came upon his body in the tall grass. He was,
thank god, alive, and I hoped he wouldn't wake and see
me see him there. The dogs and I hurried away.

But recently, when my spirits were low, and my foot was hurting from a fall with real broken bones, and I was missing my husband in a sudden fresh moment of grief, something new appeared, like a miracle. Balanced between the divided trunk of a fruit tree were a series of bone-thin sticks, like the widening strands of a delicate web, or the ribs of an unfinished boat, or an airy cradle, or a wind instrument, and nearby, another tree with the same almost invisible additions. I stopped dead in my tracks. Talk about wanting to cry out upon finding.

Of course there are the natural wonders too — the fallen branch with the head of a loon; the root that is exactly a frog, one amphibian forearm and tendril fingers grasping another root; the cobblestone caught up by a tree whose roots seem to have poured down its trunk like lava, and like lava hold the cobblestone lopsided forever. Often I see the small boy and his father who make the alphabet out of sticks on a sidewalk near the dog run; and the Tai Chi experts, like figures on a marvelous clock, who seem in their slow-motion way to be untelling time. There is the boy with a beautiful smile and strong body that I notice through the coffee shop window one Friday afternoon. The boy works for a scaffolding company and the crew is taking apart the structure that has been up so long I can't remember before. Dismantling is an art of its own, nothing is undone

The Magnificent Frigate Bird

RICH WAS A BIRDER, DYED IN THE WOOL; WE have lists from his fourth-grade sightings in Central Park. He wrote with a dark pencil and he pressed down hard. Blue jay, house finch, crow . . . Once in his twenties he sighted a Magnificent Frigate Bird off Jones Inlet, blown there by a hurricane. This was the proudest moment of his bird-watching life. On top of his dresser now are a bunch of birds, a small haphazard collection. There are the shorebirds, long-legged wading creatures; a bufflehead duck he made of clay in the seventh grade; two drab decoys we bought at an auction; a red plastic chicken (mine), which neatly lays three white eggs if you push down gently on her back; a papier-mâché crow, mascot of Old Crow, with his jaunty top hat, that I fell in love with because something in its expression reminded me of my father. There is also a little box of grain Rich saved from a cross-country trip he took when he was seventeen; he and a friend worked on farms along the way. It goes with the birds. What used to be on top of his dresser? A small tray for change, his wallet, scraps of paper with things to do, a picture of us taken at his brother's house a couple of weeks after we were married. A flashlight, just in case. A backup alarm clock, just in case. Rich was prepared for everything. He was a man who carried a couple of Band-Aids in his wallet and always had an extra hand-kerchief if somebody needed one. I've put a corn plant next to the bureau, green and leafy. They never die.

I go up to see my husband every Wednesday. My friend Ruth picks me up at eight so I get up at six in order to have the dogs walked and the paper read and the coffee drunk. It's a couple of hours north, depending on traffic, and we have become close friends over the last few months. Our destination is Kingston, and once there Ruth and I stop in Monkey Joe's, a coffee shop with fantastic cappuccino and great pumpkin muffins. We sit together for twenty minutes, then she goes to work at Benedictine Hospital and I head for the pay phone behind a Hot Wings joint that seems to be always on the verge of reopening, and call a cab to take me to the rehabilitation center where my husband has been for the past eleven months.

Sometimes when I arrive Rich is still asleep, his face relaxed, looking so like himself that I can't believe he won't wake up and be all better. Other times he is up, stalled in the middle of whatever he began to do, his back to the door, his arms raised like a conductor, motionless, as if he were playing some cosmic game of statue. Or maybe he sits on the bed, a pair of socks in one hand, his trousers laid out beside him. After our usual greeting, "Absie! How did you find me!" or "What time did you get up? I didn't hear you," he lapses back into silence. The nurses say he can stand in front of the bathroom mirror (made of shiny metal) for an hour or more, toothbrush in his hand. In brain injury jargon, perhaps this is what is meant by "difficulty completing a task."

The first time I heard this term I imagined a child who can't manage tying shoelaces, a grown-up who forgets how to scramble eggs, some kind of visible difficulty, frustration, something that could be relearned. I didn't know about the getting stuck. For my husband, there is no such thing as a minute ago, there is no *but we've been sitting here for an hour and a half.* That information has nowhere to lodge in Rich's consciousness. He has a collapsing past. If he doesn't remember, he doesn't believe. And if everything is now, what's the rush? I used to try and coax him, nudge him on (the TBI phrase is "redirect"), but that only made him angry and confused. So I have adapted. I join him. We sit and steep ourselves in 10:37, a single moment, while outside this room an hour disappears, bypassing us. I am always surprised when I look at the clock to find how long we've been there.

Once he's moving, I see how slowly he puts himself together. We select the clothes. "These aren't mine," he insists, but somehow we get past that. He puts his socks on the way he always did, rolling them back to get his toes in, unrolling them carefully over the rest of his foot, inch by inch, then pulling them over his heel. Next trousers, then shirt carefully buttoned, and everything tucked in neatly. Rich hasn't shaved in some time; instead he pulls his beard out hair by hair. This has a name but I forget what it is.

Last week he didn't smile or greet me. He wouldn't hold my hand. "What's wrong?" I asked, this was so unlike him. "We're divorced," he said, as if I were an imbecile. "We're married, Rich," I told him. "We've been married fourteen years. You're my husband," I said, touching his arm, "I'm your wife." He looked at me coldly. "Transparent windowlike words." He doesn't believe in his brain injury, so he has come up with an explanation for my absence: I have left him. "I'm alone," he says, waving his arm down the hall. "Hundreds of single beds," he says, "hundreds of single beds with old men lying in them with their boots on."

Time has gotten skewed, as tangled as fish line, what means what anymore? How could it be two years since the accident? I calculate it in months, weeks, but the numbers don't feel real or important. One hundred and four weeks. Twenty-four months. Whole handfuls of time have slipped through my fingers. Seasons rush by before I have grasped "winter," "spring." Somehow I have gotten to be sixty, in no time Rich will be seventy. We would have had parties to mark the place, but the last birthday slid by unnoticed, the last anniversary. Twenty-four months since the accident. If it were a child, it would be talking, walking, climbing into everything. "Time flaps on its mast," wrote Virginia Woolf in *Mrs. Dalloway*. For us time hangs off its mast. Sometimes I'm not even sure about the mast. Something stopped ticking April 24, 2000. Our years together ended, our future together changed. In one moment of startling clarity he told me, "My future has been dismantled." Last week he wouldn't look at me for an hour. "If I may navigate this already swollen stream of self-absorption," he said at last, "people borrow things without asking."

"What things?" I asked gratefully, and with that the subject had changed. We spent the rest of the afternoon looking at *The Sibley Guide to Birds,* which I'd bought him a year ago. We spent a long time with ducks, with woodpeckers and thrushes. He didn't recall having ever seen a Magnificent Frigate Bird and I didn't insist. Long-term memory is sometimes intact, but he'd forgotten that long-gone windy day on Long Island.

My friend Ruth, a bereavement counselor, tells me that most widows remember more vividly the last weeks of their husband's lives than the span of their lives together. I am not a widow, but my husband as he was is gone. I concentrate on who Rich is at any given moment and I lose sight of who he was, who we were. It takes my friend Denise to recall how when we had company at our house in Greenport, Rich went out early in the morning to buy several newspapers, bags of warm scones and croissants and muffins. I had forgotten, and remembering was painful. Rich used to make a mean omelet. On nights when I was cooked out and there was nothing much to eat, Rich fixed an omelet for himself. Did I want one, he always asked, and no thanks, I always said. But the look of it sliding out of the pan, perfect with that mottled brown, smelling of butter, sometimes a little lox thrown in at the last minute, weakened my resolve, and Rich would slide the better part of half onto a plate and urge me to eat. I remember how he used to wake me in Greenport with a cup of cappuccino from Aldo's. One weekend when our friends Sarah and Cornelius and Kathy were visiting we looked up the Magnificent Frigate Bird in the Audubon book and discovered that the male has a red pouch that he inflates to make himself attractive to the female, but it takes him thirty minutes to get it done. "Phoo phoo — be there in a minute, honey — phoo phoo!" We laughed ourselves sick at the kitchen table. How long ago was that? The only way to contain catastrophe is to cordon it off with dates, but the numbers mean nothing. If I think instead of how much dust would have settled on Rich's bureau, then I can feel it. There is nothing like dust.

When Rich is ready, we obtain the pass that lets us out of this locked ward and downstairs to the cafeteria. This week his mood is better, and we look forward to lunch. Rich takes the tray and passes all the baskets of condiments along the right wall. He examines carefully everything in every basket, then drops two onto the tray. Slippery packets of mayonnaise, ketchup, jelly, something unspeakably awful called "table syrup," tartar sauce, margarine, salad dressing. Soon the tray is crowded with these silvery foil-wrapped items. Napkins, two knives, two forks, two spoons. Lots and lots of saltines. I meanwhile am slapping together an egg salad sandwich for him, bowls of salad, a few bananas. We meet at the cash register. "I don't have any money," says Rich anxiously, but I tell him it's on me. (My cheese sandwich after weighing comes to thirty-two cents.) We find a table and unload the food. Last week, the week we were divorced, he looked around and said, "All these people dunking their doughnuts in a cup of sorrow, I hope it's not contaminated by the River Styx." Today we are holding hands again, happy to be together. We eat, go back for more coffee, unwrap the saltines. When the food is gone Rich starts in on the condiments, carefully opening each one, inspecting it, and scooping or squeezing out the contents and eating them on saltines. He is like a curious, determined child.

I want to be upstairs at 1:30, the designated smoking time. In the lunchroom for the Behavioral Unit, cigarettes are rationed out after mealtime, and heavy steel ashtrays gotten from the cupboard. The techs hand out the cigs and light the smokes for those who smoke, most everyone does. God knows I do. One of the patients, Mr. Mendez, has a beautiful voice and, having been asked, is now singing "The Star-Spangled Banner" in Spanish. He clasps his hands on the table, his feet tapping in time, and before each phrase he draws solemn breath from his diaphragm without compromising the pace of the anthem. He sings for fifteen minutes without coming to the end, somewhere his needle is stuck, and soon I don't know where or how the song does end. At last he finishes, or rather, stops singing. We applaud and Mr. Mendez is modest but not humble. When the clapping subsides he looks around smiling and says, "This is America." He bows.

I went to Mexico for a week last winter, a place on the Yucatán Peninsula where time stops, or at least the importance of telling time. You get up at dawn, eat when you're hungry, go to bed when it's dark. The rest of the time you lie in the sun, float in the water. There were pelicans smashing into the water in their ungainly fashion; one afternoon five impossibly pink flamingos flew by, everyone suddenly got to their feet, shielding their eyes against the sun, like a stadium full of people rising to watch a grand slam. Later I saw two other birds, and I knew what they were right away although I had never seen one before. By the time I got out my camera they had imbedded themselves higher and higher in the blue sky until they were specks. I snapped a picture but you'd never know. They could have been anything up there.

III

Learning to Live Alone

I'D HAD MY NEW CAR THREE DAYS WHEN I backed into a tree, smashing the rear window and denting the frame. The tree (ghostly in the fog) was in a hardware store parking lot, and in the car were two new garbage cans. I drove home in shock, little bits of glass tinkling in the back and no doubt dropping on the highway behind me. I pulled into the driveway of the house I'd just bought, pressed my head against the steering wheel, and waited. What was I waiting for? I was waiting for a big man to show up and fix everything. Did I mention it was raining? That the odometer had 311 miles on it?

When nobody appeared I went inside and called my children. My daughter Jennifer, perhaps speaking for them all, said kindly, "Mom, you really have to learn to drive." There seemed no point in insisting that I did know how to drive. She suggested I call the car dealer.

I did. The car dealer said, "Ouch," and suggested the auto glass company. The auto glass company suggested the bodywork man, the bodywork man said call the insurance company, which I had not yet thought to do. The insurance lady said, "Oh, let's not tell them about this. They will drop you like a hot potato." They hadn't wanted me in the first place, she assured me, a sixty-one-year-old woman who had never had car insurance, who had driven a total of zero miles in the past three years, and lived in New York City.

In the old days my husband, Rich, took care of the car. He got it inspected, changed its oil, even had the tires rotated. Had he been here I could have wailed to him about the foggy evening and the nearly invisible tree, he would have let me go upstairs and get under the covers while he took care of everything. But he wasn't here. There was just the bald fact: I had backed my car into a tree. Nothing else was relevant, the weather, the humble purchases, the small parking lot, nothing. I had backed my car into a tree, and accepting this seemed to require less energy. It turned out to be easy to open the Yellow Pages and to my delight I discovered myself capable of making the phone calls to arrange the repairs and a couple of weeks later I had my car back, almost as good as new. This small accomplishment was thrilling. Perhaps I was at last becoming an adult.

The word *capable* has always conjured up a long reach and muscled calves, perhaps a hearty laugh to go along with it—capable knew what to do with a jack, could change a fuse, rewire a lamp, but it didn't have a feminine or sexy ring to it. In the face of mechanical crises—flat tires, no hot water—I always went belly-up. Why? Because I could get away with it. Not that it's any great shakes, but I don't need a fainting couch anymore every time the house makes a terrible sound or the radiators go stone cold. If the furnace has gone off again, I flick the cellar light on, march resolutely down the stairs, stride over to my Buck Rogers spaceship of a furnace, turn a valve, and keep my eye on a glass tube that needs to fill, but not too much. Too much will result in water cascading through the ceilings. I have to do this or my pipes will burst. If I took to my bed, I might wake up in the soggy ruin of my house.

It has been almost three years since Rich's accident. I bought this house, which is only twenty minutes from where he lives. As sometimes happens with traumatic brain injury, Rich has slipped into premature dementia. I don't know what he remembers of our old life, the places we lived, the conversations we had, the routines. It's hard for me to remember what we were like before the accident, the years since have been harrowing, Rich in and out of psychosis, terrible paranoias, rages, the kinds of things brain injury sets in motion. He is calm now, he has settled comfortably into his skin, often he is merry, the rages flown, the terrors abated. Our conversations don't always make sense but they are wonderful. "You squeezed all those colors from fruit," Rich observed the other day. I was knitting a scarf out of red and purple wool. "Yes, I did," I agreed. He speaks sometimes of the "knitting lady" and the "other Abby," and if I tell him there's only one Abby and I am here right now, "Yes," he will say, then add gently, "but there's the other Abby too." And what do I know? Maybe I do have some shadowy doppelgänger in a corner of the room, or down the hall.

Doppelgängers, ghosts, my mind has always been open, which is part of the problem. Starting with the gorilla I was convinced lurked in the streets of Saint Paul when I was eleven (despite the twenty-foot snow-drifts), I've had irrational fears all my life. Back in Minnesota my father had to stand on our back porch and Mrs. Rice on her back porch, while I made the dash home after an evening of Monopoly with my friend Karen, shouting all the way. One summer Rich and I rented a small cabin in the woods of Maine—"as far from anyone else as we can get, I don't want to see another house" was my absurd criterion. It was terrible. There wasn't another living soul. When the old gent

switch controls the attic light (something I hadn't known) and turn it off. I also make it my business to go with a friend into the attic for the first time. We pull down the stairs, walk around, and I see it isn't a crawl space and there are no gargoyles, and realize it is better to see the attic than to not see the attic. There have been lots of other odd noises. First there were the wind chimes that went off with no wind, a whole bunch of them on the screened porch. I was loath to take them down lest I continue to hear them, but my youngest daughter, annoyed to tears by their incessant tinkling, cut them down willy-nilly and we haven't been troubled since. Then there was the banging that woke me and the dogs one night at one in the morning. I leapt from bed, stomped downstairs flicking on every light and yelling my head off for whoever it was to get out of my house. The hammering continued and the dogs and I were determined to track it down. Scared as I was, and I was scared, I was delighted to find that anger overrode my fear. I was not going to cower in my bedroom or hide in my closet. I was going to beard the lion in its den. And, anyway, it was my den. Whenever we got close, the noise stopped, then started up again somewhere else. "This is my house," I shouted down the cellar stairs at one point (the only time my dogs were really scared). Eventually we lay down on the couch, every light in the house blazing, and waited it out. Later my friend Chuck suggested he get me a chain saw as a housewarming present. I could keep it under my pillow. The sight of me in my big flannel nightie carrying a chain saw would surely scare the bejesus out of anything. For the record, I never found out what made the hammering but happily it hasn't come back.

I'm comfortable here. The sound of something smacking its lips over by the fireplace? I don't even look up from my knitting. A kind of slithery sound like something being (gasp) dragged? A sound that morphs into heavy breathing (through a very large nose) that comes, upon investigation, from the walls of every single room in the house? No problem. If I don't hear toenails scrabbling, and I don't, the dogs and I go to bed. The noises are real and no doubt have a logical explanation, but at midnight logic is not my companion, so the solution is to keep my imagination in check. A warm body on either side of me under the covers is excellent company and I find a big smile on my face, thinking that we are coexisting with walls that snuffle and grunt. In the old days I'd've been out of the house in a microsecond, but had I left, I might never have been able to come back.

I KNOW WHAT I'M DOING HERE. I LOVE THE HOUSE, the village, the people I've met are already dear to me.

And Rich is only twenty minutes away. Today he is unshaven, walking slowly into the lunchroom when I arrive. He is wearing wrinkled khaki trousers and an unfamiliar flannel shirt that his daughter, Sally, must have brought him. He looks at me with surprise and happiness. "Absie!" he says. His hands are cold. He is sweetness itself. His hug still warms me like nothing else. We go downstairs to the art room, passing the huge goldfish tank. Usually he comments on how fat the goldfish are, but today he stops. "I wonder if they know where they are," he says. "Or if they remember other aquariums."

In the middle of the night I think of his smiling face, and the goblins disperse. Or if they don't, I can stare them down.

How to Break Up a Dogfight

GRAB THE HAUNCHES OF THE SMALLER DOG and pull. Or grab the haunches of the larger dog and pull. Forget about being bitten. Or consider what your friend Claudette did in this situation and recall her words for their comic relief. "I screamed and threw a paper towel at them."

Carry a water pistol at all times filled with some repellent liquid. Try to remember the name of the harmless substance all dogs hate. Toy with the idea of ammonia, lemon juice. Tear gas. Wear an earsplitting whistle around your neck. Have handy a coffee can filled with coins to shake at them. Shock yourself by declaring after a fight in which your hound, Carolina, bit her own tongue and sent streams of blood flying at your skirt, "I feel just like Jackie Kennedy." Ponder your sudden ability to joke about the event that for forty years had you weeping every time you thought of it. Try to figure out why this is no longer sacred ground. Realize that September 11 changed everything.

Hire a dog trainer and then be unavailable for the next three months through no fault of your own. Make sure that for the initial visit you have hurt your back and can't move anything except your eyes and mouth without screaming. After he leaves remember everything you did badly as a mother and begin to get depressed. Have a falling-out with a beloved daughter and get so depressed you can't see straight. Call your psychiatrist after a year and discover she is out of town for the next three weeks. Listen to your friend who suggests you think about whether dogfights and family fights have any similarities and if you can apply what you have learned about one to the other. Realize that you know nothing about either and can do nothing about anything. The next time the dogs start growling and circling each other, fling open the kitchen door and stomp down the steps shouting, "If you don't stop that this minute I am leaving forever and never coming back!" Face the fact that this is probably not the first time these words escaped your lips. Think about your children's childhoods and fall further into a slough of despond.

Try another approach. At the earliest sign of an escalating growl, get up and leave the room. This is called *removing yourself from the equation* and try to remember what this has to do with mathematics. Fail. Discover that when you are gone they lose interest in fighting, and wonder whether everything is always all your fault. Enjoy a pointless thought about the tree falling in the forest. Notice and begin to appreciate the fact that dogs do not apologize. When the altercation is complete, they head across the bright green lawn tails high, bumping sides as they run. Lament the human addiction to apologies, and how easily they are botched. Be prepared when you hear from your estranged daughter. Be jubilant cautiously.

Try not to read too much into the news that she has just bought a dog.

Dog Talk

ROSIE NEEDED TO PLAY, AND I WASN'T UP TO it. I'd grown weary of running after her to give up a soggy ball I didn't want in the first place, and she had no receptors for "drop it." Poor Harry stood stoically while Rosie ran around him barking, nipping his hind legs to give him a jump start. All in vain. She deserved an equal, and I looked at several dogs who needed homes: a rambunctious big black Lab mix who would have overwhelmed us; a pretty blue-eyed husky who hated men; a tiny little thing that looked like a silver eyebrow running around the house but Harry growled and snapped and that was that—the allergic owner swept her up in his arms and out they went. One rainy night I almost adopted a pregnant Dalmatian. The pet store owners offered to pay her vet bills and help with adoption of the puppies, they were so desperate to find her a home. I didn't ask the circumstances of her being knocked up, but the deed had been done, they told me, by a cocker spaniel. Elvina lay on the floor of Dog-a-Rama, raising her head with only minimal interest when stroked gently along her spine. She was in a fix and she knew it. The pet store owners were nice men with accents I couldn't place. They were visibly upset. People were interested in a free Dalmatian, they told me, but not a pregnant one.

I was about to teach my night class around the corner, and although I had nothing against bringing her to school, something stayed my hand. I had to think this through. Could I protect her? What if my exuberant Rosie wanted her to get up and play? What if Harry took a dislike to her puppies? When I was a girl, our dachshund, Max, ate a litter of kittens. Could I keep the babies safe? My class, when polled, was 100 percent for adoption—but they were writers, and writers suggest things just to see what happens next. My friends were more cautious, one of them laughing as if the words "a pregnant Dalmatian" were the punch line of an excellent joke. I got home at midnight and called my daughter Jen, who to my surprise was not encouraging. "Not a great idea, Ma," she said. I telephoned the store the following afternoon and learned Elvina had found a home.

Hallelujah.

And then a friend called. "You should go see this dog," Susan said. "I hear she's wonderful. I think she's some kind of beagle." So I called Jodi Judson and went for a visit. *You ain't nuthin but a hound dog,* I all but sang when I first laid eyes on her.

Carolina Bones was gangly and goofy, with a lugubrious expression that gave her a kind of ridiculous dignity. One look at her loping around the yard and I was in love. Jodi had found the dog living at a rest stop off I-95 somewhere in South Carolina. She was so skinny that her bones were working holes through her skin. Jodi says she thinks Carolina was near death that night, because she could barely stand. Jodi fed her all the food she and her husband had, but they were on their way back from vacation, and her husband was reluctant to take a strange dog in their car for the fourteen-hour trip ("Don't even think about it," he said) and they drove away. Jodi says she didn't say a word, but when they crossed the state line her husband said, "Oh, all right," and turned the car around.

These days all I talk about is dogs. For a while it was dogs and my poor health but I'm better so it's back to just dogs. I get nervous when I find myself answering the question "What's new?" by eagerly detailing the sleeping arrangements of the previous night—whether the four of us slept in the same bed or did Rosie go once again into the guest room. Sometimes I detect the tiniest pause before whoever it is murmurs a change of subject, then remembers an errand. But my dogs make me laugh, and they comfort me, and I'm never bored with them. When Rosie's head lies on my shoulder, Harry crams himself into my left side, and Carolina curls up like something folded by a Chinese laundry, impossibly small and neat, I am perfectly happy. We are the peaceable kingdom on a double bed. This is what it must have been like before the apple, when everything had a name but there wasn't so much discussion. I once asked my eldest daughter, Sarah, the mother of five, what it was about dogs that made loving them so easy. "They don't talk," she said.

They do communicate. When Carolina arrived there was the need to establish a pecking order. For the first week it was mostly a dog version of cussing, then one afternoon Rosie and Carolina had a fight, and when it was over Carolina's ear was bitten through. As I tended to the bleeding, I realized that like it or not, I was right in the middle of a wild and natural process. I was a card-carrying member of an animal pack, and to top it off, I was the alpha dog. I was the alpha dog, and the privilege of who sat next to me where, when, and how close, was up for grabs. Rosie triumphed over

Carolina that afternoon, although she was the smaller dog.

It's simpler than what humans go through. "Your voice sounds funny, are you mad at me?" a young woman speaks anxiously, cell phone pressed to ear, and I wonder how people ever manage to hook up. Dogs are never in a bad mood over something you said at breakfast. Dogs never sniff at the husks of old conversations, or conduct autopsies on weekends gone wrong. An unexamined life may not be worth living, but the overexamined life is hell. We talk too much.

A friend is visiting, and he has fallen asleep on the sofa. Carolina, leery of him from the git-go, is terrified when a book falls from his lap and hits the floor, and he wakes up with a jolt. "Was that me?" he asks, looking around. I nod. Carolina can't stop trembling. Harry loves my friend and Rosie leaps up for kisses, so it's not like he gives off bad vibes. I wish he'd get a dog. He isn't married anymore, and his life seems lonesome. He is my funniest, wisest, oldest pal.

"Have you ever considered suicide?" I asked years ago, when we were both still young enough to be talking about life and death. It was probably 1978.

"Of course," he replied, between bites of hot turkey sandwich.

"How would you do it?" I asked.

"I've always rather fancied hacking my own head off," he said. I was drinking coffee and laughed so hard it came out my nose.

"Difficult," I said, when I could speak again.

"That's the point," he said. "You wouldn't want it to be easy."

That's when I knew I would love him forever.

He arrived yesterday evening, after a late start. He probably almost didn't come. He has difficulty, he says, visiting friends. I notice he is happiest when he has spent enough time to qualify as a satisfactory house-guest—a night, a morning, most of an afternoon. Knowing he can leave any time now and not seem rude, he relaxes, dillydallies, engages in less workmanlike conversations. He reminds me of somebody standing next to the edge of the cliff after making the dangerous climb. He isn't going to stay, but he can peek at it.

"I think you should buy a house up here," I say. We are sitting in my backyard.

"That sounds nice," he says.

"You could come over for coffee all the time."

"And go into work three days a week," he says, as if he's actually considering it. The pretense is a courtesy, but I appreciate good manners.

"You could have a dog," I continue. It's a lovely evening, he's getting ready to go.

"I could," he says.

The dogs churn around his ankles like surf when he says good-bye. I wave, I don't press him to stay. Then I close the door. "Naptime," I announce, and my pack and I scramble toward the sofa, where we will doze for a good long while, piled on top of each other like a bunch of puppies.

How to Banish Melancholy

YOU WILL NEED THREE DOGS, ONE OF WHOM has caught the scent of something interesting wafting through the second-floor window. She is a hound. They are all hounds and the four of you sleep together on a double bed. When you open your eyes (her warm doggy breath on your face) she will be staring at you with such intensity that you burst out laughing. You will throw on yesterday's clothes (which are lying conveniently on the floor) and head downstairs without tripping over Rosie, Harry, or Carolina, all of whom are underfoot. When you open the kitchen door they will fly into the yard and immediately commence hunting, noses to the ground, some small creature whose zigzagging trail resembles an electrocardiogram. You follow them onto the wet green lawn. So now you're outdoors and it's five A.M.

For the last month you've been inside while it rained. Perhaps you are a fan of rain, but this may have gone on too long. You have stopped answering your phone. You don't gather the mail. You have noticed that bad as it was when two dogs followed you from room to room, it's even worse with three. Every time you get up, they get up. *Please don't, it's not worth it,* you want to say as you rise from your soft red chair to wander into the kitchen on an errand you forget before arriving. You look out the window while the dogs settle down on a rug by the stove. They are so good-natured. Moments later you drift into the living room and again the dogs trail along behind, and if you do this often enough, the aimlessness of your day is driven home. From here it is but a hop, skip, and a jump to the pointlessness of your existence, which is why it is so excellent to be outdoors with your clothes on at five this morning.

Next, you will need a bed of nettles five feet high. Perhaps you already have a garden like this, having neglected it for the two years you have lived in the country. You have told yourself that you don't want to put anything into the ground so you will not have to hate the deer who will certainly eat it, but the fact is you are bone lazy and prefer drinking coffee and sitting on the stoop to weeding or raking or digging a hole. But nettles have closed over the heads of three pink peony bushes you could swear you saw two summers ago, and you are experiencing an unfamiliar surge of energy. You dash inside and good, there they are, the gardening gloves given to you as a housewarming present two years ago still stapled together. You rip them apart, don them, and charge back into the yard.

Your first nettle comes up with the perfect amount of resistance — none — you can yank it out by the roots and you do so, flinging it with joy behind you. You yank another and another, and pretty soon you are a madwoman, pulling nettles three at a time, caring nothing for the stinging on your arms and ankles, and the mound grows on the grass behind you. Sometimes you get a stubborn old grandfather and pulling as hard as you can you reach the big root snaking just under the surface and you get that too, dirt flying as you tear it out, and now you are *the old woman and the nettle,* destroyer and giver of life, and you understand the ferocity of the gardener.

After five or six minutes you will tire and stand back from your work. A tiny patch has been thinned. Perhaps you will now make coffee and bring the cup outside. If all goes well, a perfect pink peony bush will be revealed by lunchtime. There will be slim yellow irises too, and the big throaty purple ones that remind you, alas, of an old man's scrotum, but you will weed there too. By early afternoon the sun may burn through what has been a heavy mist, and should you not be ready to be dazzled, do not fret. It is time for a nap anyway. Inside you may notice that what you thought was dust is instead a layer of golden pollen blowing through the open windows. *If only life were more like this,* you will think, as you and the dogs traipse up to bed, and then you realize with a start that this *is* life.

Carolina's in Heat and I'm Not

M Y HOUND DOG, CAROLINA, IS SITTING IN THE car, and I'm in the drugstore standing in an aisle I haven't been down for fifteen years. Carolina is in heat. Such an archaic concept, heat. I'm looking for something to slip into the mesh pocket of a red Speedo-like contraption I've just bought for her. Who knew they made such things for dogs? I recall the flimsy little garter belts we girls got with our first box of sanitary napkins and the accompanying pamphlet regarding the human reproductive cycle. Light years ago. I pick an item that comes wrapped in pink and says mini and then I hobble over to Aisle 4b, Pain Relievers, where I'm more at home. My back hurts. I grab aspirin, pay for everything, and head for the car. Carolina's nose is smeared against the window. "Good dog," I say, "good dog," and manage to get myself sitting down without screaming and I pat her big head and nuzzle her neck, and her tail thwacks against the passenger seat. Carolina is halfway through her first treatment for heartworm and going into heat seems grossly unfair. "Jesus, yet more trouble," as some martyr said when the executioner reached in to yank out his intestines. (I can't remember which saint this was, but my mother loved to quote him.) Before I start the car I line up the arrows, take off the cap, stab a pen through the foil seal, and gobble down three aspirin.

This is my first experience with a dog in heat but the back pain arrived thirty years ago when I bent to pick a canned peach off the kitchen floor and couldn't straighten up. My second husband seemed familiar with the problem. "My god, what is this called?" I cried as he tried to help. "It's called my back is killing me," he said. This version of my back is killing me comes from wearing a pair of stylish new red shoes that pinch my left foot and make me walk lopsided. I don't know why I keep putting them on except they show off my ankles. At age sixty-three, ankles are my best feature unless you count cake.

When I get home I discover it's nearly impossible to put this thing on my dog. There is a place for her tail and Velcro fastenings that go over her haunches but try sticking a dog's long tail through the hole of a small slippery garment while the dog turns around and around in circles. It takes fifteen minutes and when I succeed, Carolina turns her baleful eyes on me and I want to apologize. She is a dog dressed like a monkey.

The next morning I can barely walk. My friend Claudette comes to the rescue. She puts Carolina on a leash lest a pack of hormone-addled canines show up in my yard, and later she drives me to her acupuncturist. I have never been to an acupuncturist but I'm ready for help here. The process is very interesting, all those needles tingling in my feet and legs and hands, and so relaxing that I would probably doze off were it not for the needle stuck right under my nose. I just can't stop thinking about that one. Nevertheless I do feel better until I hit the dairy case at the Hurley Ridge Market and reach for half a gallon of milk. On the way back through town we drive past the half-dressed youth of Woodstock lying on the village green. They are a beautiful sight, but what with my bad back and good memory I am glad not to be one of them. They have far too much future.

Meanwhile, my fat beagle, Harry, has found himself capable of leaping straight up into the air like Rudolf Nureyev. If Carolina doesn't notice, and she doesn't, he does it again. He is no longer capable of reproducing, but that doesn't dampen his spirit. Rosie too is affected by whatever hormones are flying. She engages in much vigorous grooming, attending obsessively to the nooks and crannies of both Harry and Carolina. She would have made an excellent mother. Now and then Carolina rouses herself long enough to emit a howl. Everybody's getting hot around here except me. I am just beginning to wonder where all the would-be suitors are when a big white dog materializes in the driveway. Ha! Carolina's first admirer. Harry and Rosie take up their positions on the back porch barking their heads off and I call my sister Judy and tell her proudly we've got an intact husky hanging around who probably never finished grammar school. "Now you know how Mom and Dad felt," she says. I go outside holding Carolina's leash in one hand, and a mop in the other. The mop doubles as cane and threat, and I shake it at the ruffian when he comes too close. He looks at Carolina and she looks back. Oh yeah, I remember that look. If this animal were human he'd be wearing jeans and a white T-shirt. He'd be lighting a cigarette. Forget my bad back, my advanced years. If this animal were human and I were in Carolina's shoes, let's face it, I'd be all over him like white on rice.

For Now

LAST OCTOBER WHEN MY FURNACE BROKE and the weather got cold and colder, when I woke up and the temperature inside the bedroom was forty degrees or thirty-eight degrees, when the dogs and I stayed under the covers until our bladders were bursting, I vowed never to forget, never again to take heat for granted. But I did forget. And now it's summer and the electricity is out. My red slipcovers are soaking in the stalled washing machine while my furniture sits around in its underwear. I can't run the vacuum cleaner or have toast. One minute I was knitting, the radio on, the fan blowing in my face, and the next minute everything went still. I have not got to where I vow to remember this. But we don't get to choose what sticks. How many times I have run my fingers along a picket fence and thought, "This! I will remember this moment always!" and all that remains is the memory of a desire to hold on to a memory. My uncle told me that every fall the dragonflies in Brazil return to the lake where they were born to touch down once more before dying. I have taken it on myself to remember this for him.

I DON'T LIKE IT WHEN SOMEBODY REMEMBERS something I love better than I do. There are places I don't often mention lest somebody remember more than I do—Sneden's Landing, say, where we lived for a few years in the 1950s. My sister Judy had more friends, and she has a better memory, and when she turns on her brights I stand exposed, stripped of detail, unworthy to have lived there at all. But I remember streams we followed downhill to the river, and where we once searched for a plant with a silver leaf and thick juicy stems which cured poison ivy. What its name was, whether we found any, and who had poison ivy I can't recall. I remember a beautiful dark waterfall and the deep pool it fell into, and the columns and grape arbor that stood around. If you put your foot in the icy water you went numb up to your knee. I remember the Hudson at low tide and finding treasures in the smelly mud, once a smooth piece of carved jade and lots of broken china. I remember lying on a jetty that extended off

Should my sister say she loves wisteria, that wisteria is her favorite flower, part of me wants to shout, "It grew outside MY window." But none of it belongs to me.

My god, Tony was a handsome boy. He had no curfew and a Nash Rambler and I could hear it coming from forty miles way. He invited me out, but at fifteen I was scared and shy, and five minutes before he was due to pick me up I'd beg my mother to tell him I was sick. Finally I went to his house for supper. I can't remember anything except the Ovaltine, which I was afraid to drink for fear the Haitian cook had put a voodoo spell on it. I've got a photograph of me with Tony printed on a matchbook from the Copacabana, where we went one night with his parents. He was seventeen and I was sixteen. My sister kept the matchbook safe for me for forty years. Then she handed it over. My eldest daughter framed it in a silver frame and gave it to me for Christmas as a surprise. In this photo you can see dark shadows under his eyes. My eyes look black—my pupils opening wide in the flash of the camera.

"How is Rich?" people ask. "Does he remember you?" Yes, he knows me and his daughter, Sally. He knows his granddaughter, Nora. The four of us spend Thursday afternoons together. Sally and the baby come down from Albany and I pick Rich up at the nursing home and drive him to my house in Woodstock. These days he seems to recognize sights along Route 28. Or does he? Maybe it's just his funny bone that's tickled when we pass the sign for Thomas's Pest Control, because he chuckles every time. Sometimes he remarks, "Here we are," when the church comes up on our left and we make the turn. "Hello, Shorty," he says to Harry, our old dog.

I don't know what happened to all Rich's memories. One of his favorites was the cool birch woods in Finland, where he once ran a race, a place he used to conjure up whenever he felt in a tight spot. He is very hard of hearing now, and that much conversation would be almost impossible. "Do you remember the woods in Finland?" I would have to shout, and then watch him struggle to hear, and then to make sense of what I said. Sometimes that is too sad. Besides, there is enough going on. "Do you want to use the bathroom?" Sally suggested to her father last week. He shook his head and asked, "Why? Do you have a dire need for fresh urine?" We laughed, and I wrote it down so I don't forget.

After lunch Rich always takes his old place by the sink and begins to wash the dishes. No part of him has forgotten the slow circling of the sponge on the face of the plate, or the careful rinsing of glasses or cleaning between the tines of a fork. When Sally and the baby leave to go home, Rich and I hold hands and wave good-bye from the porch. Later he will put on his reading glasses and take up the paper. The dogs will deposit themselves near our feet. The afternoon will slide into evening, and before it gets dark I will take him back to the place where he lives, but not yet. For now, he will look at the paper and I will look at him, and let what's over and done with disappear into the here and now.

IV

Filling What's Empty

AN OLD REFRIGERATOR CAME WITH THE house. It contained a half bottle of ketchup, a squeeze container of ballpark mustard, and an open jar of pickle relish. I appreciate how hard it is to throw such things away, and harder still to pack them up and move them with you, but other people's condiments are depressing. On top of that, unidentified odors leaked into the freezer; if you pulled out a vegetable drawer a shelf collapsed; and the outside was made of some wrinkled Naugahyde-like material you can't clean. (I don't know who invented this stuff, but it was surely not the hand that holds the sponge.) Anyway, I just never warmed up to this appliance, and I blamed it for the fact that except for Thanksgiving I never bought food. So two years later, armed with statistics from *Consumer Reports*, I marched off to Sears and three days after that, a brand-new, spanking clean appliance arrived in my kitchen.

THIS NEW BABY GLEAMS. THE STAINLESS STEEL EXterior cost extra and it came with a bottle of special cleaner and instructions in three languages. The vegetable drawers have choices for degrees of crispness. The door can hold two half-gallon containers of milk side by side, the freezer is spacious and smells only of cold. There is even a separate shelf for eggs. The first week I bought yogurt and cottage cheese and apples and chicken and lettuce and cream. I had milk and orange juice and seltzer, and for my visiting daughter and her friends, beer. I even put water in the ice cube trays. I invited friends for supper and made my mother's famous potatoes—Gruyère cheese, heavy cream, red-hot pepper flakes, salt and pepper, nutmeg. And oh yes, potatoes. I made hot fudge sauce and stocked up on four pints of vanilla ice cream. And then a week went by and another and now the icebox is empty again. You won't find the makings of a ham and cheese sandwich, or even peanut butter and jelly. There's precious little in the way of greenery although a head of iceberg lettuce has stayed unnaturally crisp for several weeks in the vegetable drawer. I try to make up grocery lists but never get very far. I do always have coffee and dog food

(I love to buy dog food) and usually there's a pound of butter in the freezer. But I can't blame my poor shopping habits on the refrigerator anymore, this new one is begging to be filled.

Maybe it's because I'm a WASP. This reminds me of the cookbook I started to write years ago. It was to be a WASP cookbook and I was going to call it *The Goy of Cooking*. In a preface I never finished I noted that WASPs are not bad cooks, and we have lots of great recipes (think *popovers,* think *standing rib roast,* think *fudge*). Our problem lies in the fact that we never buy food. I abandoned the project, and never got to the bottom of this failing. (A friend offered me Marianne Moore's recipe for custard. I thanked her and said I had a recipe for custard already. "Oh but this is very WASPy," she went on. "It's custard *for one.*") On the other hand, when my kids were small my refrigerator was far from empty. I remember a lot of yogurt, cream cheese, jelly, peanut butter, American cheese slices, cheddar cheese, Roquefort, leftover apple pie (if there were leftovers), leftover brisket, apples, orange juice, butter, milk. Lettuce and tomatoes and onions and potatoes. For a while my freezer contained a bottle of vodka with a wisp of buffalo grass inside, and for a few bad years I took swigs of this syrupy concoction all day long.

———

STILL, THE WASP THEORY DIES HARD. I HAVE ONLY to remember taking my old friend Jerry to my mother's house in East Hampton. I heard a cry from the kitchen and went to see what was wrong. He was standing in front of the open refrigerator, pointing to its contents—a bottle of champagne and a jar of bitter marmalade, both sitting on doilies. And then there's the memory of my mother's frantic cry when any of us children headed toward the kitchen. "Don't eat anything!" In her later years as a great grandmother she plied us all with baked Brie and pâté and cookies. She broke off big pieces of chocolate bar beseeching us to eat. In the old days perhaps she had bought only enough food to last through supper. Maybe what we were eating were the ingredients of the evening meal. She was a good cook but sometimes meat was on the chewy side. On these occasions she glared at us as we valiantly gnawed our way through strips of beef. "Good tough meat," she would say in a challenging tone.

At the same time my refrigerator arrived I collapsed the dining room table and lined the walls with bookcases. I don't have a dining room sort of life—we eat on our laps in the kitchen if I have company—and this was a room I passed through to get somewhere else. It was useless, really, except for Thanksgiving. And now we're headed into fall, my favorite season, and there are empty bookcases all around me, and boxes of books in New York City waiting to be moved up here. I sit in this new room, trying it on for size, and discover that my house doesn't fit me anymore. Maybe it's because from here I can see into the empty kitchen, and then turn my head and look into the empty living room. On either side are these uninhabited rooms, quiet, waiting, but only for me, and I can't sit everywhere at once.

It occurs to me that eating is a social occasion. Living alone I don't have the energy for shopping, for cooking meals. The dogs and I do fine with me eating standing up and dropping bits of my makeshift supper—often this is buttered toast—into their mouths. But Rich comes on Thursdays, and Sally with Nora, and we have lunch together. Rich lost his sense of smell with the accident, and with it much of his ability to taste. Of all the catastrophic losses he suffered this one seemed gratuitous, and just plain mean. We'd had our favorite meals—baby flounder fried in butter and oil, which we ate with new potatoes and peas; home fries on a rainy afternoon. All this past winter I roasted chickens for Thursdays, or made omelets, but summer has been hot, and nowadays it's mostly deli takeout. Rich still loves to eat, but I don't know what he tastes.

This Thursday he was anxious. A new doctor had taken him off two of his medications—why do they mess with what works?—and when I went to pick him up he was agitated and miserable, he couldn't come with me, he had plans, there were things he had to do. I wondered if he thought he was back at work. For a couple of years after his accident, he would get desperate, believing he was supposed to be covering a news story he couldn't remember. "We can do everything in Woodstock," I said, but no, no, he had to stay, if he left now nothing would get done and he couldn't put it off any longer. He was sitting on the chair in his little room; a copy of the new *American Heritage Dictionary* I'd given him was on the bed. "Let's go," I said. "Sally is waiting with the baby," but to no effect. He stood up and felt in his pockets. "I'm looking for something and I don't know what it is. I won't even know it when I find it," he said.

How did I convince him to leave with me? A mix of cajoling and bullying. We got to the house, where Sally and Nora were waiting, and he was happy to see them as he always is. We ate our big sandwiches and Rich had a couple of chocolate chip cookies, his favorite, but he didn't want coffee, which was just as well since there was no milk.

"I've got to go," he said, getting up. "It's late." Sally and I looked at each other. We were only an hour into a lovely afternoon. Nora was eating Cheerios in her playpen, the dogs were sleeping in the sun, but Rich was headed for the door, determined to leave. All business.

There was a new notebook on the counter. I'd bought it because of the color—a wonderful red, and for the green planets on its cover. I handed this to Rich, found a pen, and coaxed him back to the chair. "Here," I said, "you can get organized. Write all the things you need to do." He sat back down and leaning the notebook against his knee he began immediately to write. He looked like a reporter again. Was he thinking about camera crews and soundmen? Was he laying out procedures? The longer he wrote the more curious I got and finally I stood behind the chair and looked over his shoulder.

"Corn for corn soup. Lettuce, cucumber for salad, along with tomatoes and some cheddar cheese. Kaliber and orange juice. Milk too. Apple juice too. Thicken sliced sandwich bread. Tuna fish, sardines, onions, ham, sardines. Crackers for the cheese."

NO

i

HERE IS HOW I GET MY HUSBAND IN THE car: I lie.

"I'm going to buy us something for dinner. Will you come with me?"

This rainy October afternoon I stick a fake log in the fireplace and light it and we spend what Rich used to call the shank of the day in each other's company, dozing and waking to firelight. It is like being married again. But he can't stay. Sooner or later I have to get up from my chair and disturb him. I have to touch his arm, speak in his ear, jostle him. I have to coax him out of his warm chair and into the car so I can drive him back. "I'm going to get us something for dinner. Will you come with me?" This is what I hate: that he nods so willingly and gets to his feet. That it works every time.

The dogs allow themselves to be corralled in the living room and Rich and I go slowly down the back steps, my arm under his left arm, his right hand on the banister. I am carrying a box of cookies and once he has gotten into the passenger seat and I've stretched the seat belt and he has buckled it, I give them over. "Chocolate chippers! I might have to have one," he says, opening the box. We are headed back to the Northeast Center for Special Care. I am trying not to feel anything. Now that we are on our way, I want to get it over with. I want to get him there and safely up to his room, then I want to leave as fast as I can. "Are we going to two markets?" Rich asks and I nod. But we drive past the Black Bear Deli and the Hurley Ridge Market without him noticing. We drive down Route 28, we pass the K&R Car Wash, and the single-story pink building that houses Catskill Mountain Organic Coffee, which roasts its own beans, we pass Thomas's Pest Control (Got Mice? Not Nice!) and take the turn for Route 209 North, and I hold my breath waiting to see if this time he will latch on to the fact that I am betraying him. Out of the corner of my eye I can see his hands around the container of cookies on his lap. I am trying not to feel anything.

"It's been a lovely three days," says Rich, and I know he thinks we're on vacation. "What are our plans?" he asks. "Are we looking for a motel?" He is happy. I remember vacations. We were good companions. I remember the island of Nevis, where little birds ate sugar out of the bowls on our breakfast table. Rich took long runs down the beach and I read *Howards End,* inexplicably bursting into tears at the end. We had lobster salad sandwiches and fell in love with pelicans and wondered what living there all the time would be like.

When we get to the nursing home Rich wants to leave the cookies in the car.

"How will they know these are ours?" he asks. "They will think we are stealing."

"I will tell them as soon as we go in," I say, and grab the box over his protests and hold his arm, steering us through the parking lot. I smile at the man who opens the sliding glass doors, and Rich's electronic bracelet sets off the alarm briefly. "Hello, Mr. Rogin," he says. "Did you have a nice day?" but Rich is hard of hearing. We make our way to the elevator.

"What button should I push?" he asks.

"Two," I say.

How do I live with myself?

Some of the residents are in the big dining room watching a movie with Goldie Hawn, but I bring Rich to his room, where I tell myself he will be comfortable. His single bed is neatly made, some of his clothes are folded on top—underwear, two sweatshirts. I gesture toward the chair. "Why don't you sit down for a minute," I suggest. "I will be back soon. I'm going to run a couple of errands." I try not to register his bewildered expression. "I will be back soon."

I notice the plants need watering but I'll do it next time.

"But what do we want?" my husband asks. He is distressed, and I realize that I am in his room at the nursing home with one foot out the door, but he is in the supermarket.

"Milk," I say.

"Just milk?" He seems dubious.

"Just milk."

"How much milk?"

"Half a gallon," I say, pushing the box of cookies into his hands. I know in five minutes he'll forget I was there at all. I kiss him. Then I'm gone.

ONCE I STOOD IN LINE BEHIND A YOUNG WOMAN ORDERing coffee who remarked to her friend that she didn't yet have a set of beliefs, and I imagined catalogs from which one could order such sets, like furniture, beliefs that wouldn't collapse under one's full weight, big sturdy reliable sideboards of belief. As for me, I have learned what I can do and what I can't. I know my limits. That's all I have to go on, but it's better than nothing.

ii

IT'S A RAINY NIGHT IN 1987 AND I'M COMING OUT
of the West Side Market with a pint of heavy cream and
two boxes of strawberries. My fourteen-year-old daughter and I have been eating strawberry shortcake for almost two weeks now. "It's fruit," I tell myself, "vitamin
C," as I maniacally roll out the biscuit dough night after
night. Anyway, this particular night there is Crystal, only
I don't know her yet. I notice a tall woman wearing an
army jacket several sizes too big. She isn't saying anything; you really don't need to if you're standing on the
sidewalk with a bunch of kids and a big pregnant belly
and you're holding your right hand out, palm up. A little
boy stands behind her, his face buried in her jacket. I
think of my grandsons and I'm having one of those
shocks you get, here is someone I'm meant to know,
and I scrounge around in my pockets and ask if there's
anything else she needs. "I don't have much money but
I've got lots of stuff," I say. "Do you need anything
else?" She smiles. She has a beautiful calm face. "Thank
you," she says in a soft voice, and she shows her kids
the twenty I have just thrust in her palm.

"Plates," she says, turning back to me. "We have a
place to live but we don't have plates."

Well, I've got plates and I go home and pack some

up in a box along with forks and spoons and knives and some extra mugs. I add a huge jar of honey and carry the box back to where they are still standing. I insist on giving her cab fare and she and the kids pile into the car and go home with booty. For the next month I run into Crystal maybe once a week, usually outside the market, and for some reason, we really hit it off. Sometimes we go have coffee at Happy Burger and talk about music or fled youth; we compare women with children to women without and agree they don't speak our language. Then she gives birth and I don't see her for a while. A few months later she is outside the West Side Market with Jeremiah and Goldie, and we all have lunch together in Happy Burger, and I try not to notice that both kids smell of urine, and that this four-year-old boy has never learned to talk. Crystal and I sit with our elbows on the table and we talk about childbirth and laugh about men. I love her resilience, her optimism, her sense of humor. The hardest part about asking for money, she says, is that it is embarrassing. I want to know what she has learned about human nature. "People don't stop when it's raining," she says, with a laugh. One night we go see *Predator* together, both of us love Arnold, and after the cab drops her off the driver asks, "Is she your maid?" and I say, "No," righteously, "she is my friend."

But it isn't true. There is a dividing line. I am careful with Crystal to say only what I mean, not to exag-
gerate. Her life scares me. There have been injuries to
her children, the eldest in particular, her arm broken in
some disciplinary action taken about an open window.
"It wasn't Ray's fault," says Crystal, "it was an accident,"
and I look at the girl who says nothing, stares at the
table. Crystal has another family of grown children in
Florida, but she mentions their existence only once, and
she hasn't seen them in twelve years. Her husband used
to smoke crack, she finally tells me, but he's clean now.

Then one day there is Crystal and all eight kids—
she has eight now, the pregnancy was twins—waiting
for me outside my work. The children look tired and
grimy. Crystal is nervous. She is perspiring. "I told them
to be quiet and to put on all their underwear this morning," she says. "I decided on the spur of the moment."
Ray is smoking crack, and she isn't going to go through
that again. She is taking the children and going tomorrow to Tuskegee, where she has heard they are good to
strangers. They've been all day at a park far from their
neighborhood, and they need a place to sleep. The bus
leaves in the morning. Can they stay at my apartment?

"Of course," I say.

Catherine isn't pleased, these are the kids who ate
her special Italian lollipop, the one she had been saving

for two years; it had a design inside like a flower. She isn't happy, but she knows there is no choice. "What can I say, Mom? No, you can't stay here with your kids, you have to sleep on a bench?" They arrive, we order pizza, everyone is fed, and the kids run around. It's as if my apartment is full of little wildfires, and I can't put them all out, the floor is burning. Finally I tell Crystal that Catherine and I are going to the movies. Crystal is going through a bag of children's clothes that my eldest daughter has given me for her. "Have a good time," she says, smiling.

"Maybe when we get back they'll all be asleep," I say to my daughter.

"But, Ma, it's like *we* don't have a home," Catherine says as we walk downtown to the Olympia. When we return the children are sleeping. They are everywhere, draped over the arms of chairs, the back of the sofa, under the coffee table, on the rug, on the bare floor. They look like little birds who have been shot out of the sky, all lying where they fell. Crystal is asleep in the rocker and Catherine and I tiptoe past, and I ask if Catherine wants to come in my bed and she does, and neither of us sleep. "What if they don't leave?" she whispers, but I am already afraid of that.

Crystal moves slowly the next morning. Socks are carefully chosen from those sorted out of the bag, shoes are tied carefully; everyone wears something new, everyone has their hair brushed, everyone washes their face and brushes their teeth. I stand around mentally wringing my hands, sneaking peeks at the clock. What if they miss the bus? What if she asks to stay longer? Whatever this is a test of, I'm not passing it. Finally they are ready to set off. Crystal carries a suitcase I give her that contains the rest of the hand-me-down clothes from my daughter's family.

"I was afraid you'd miss the bus," I say, hoping I don't sound relieved. They have fifty-five minutes to get to Port Authority.

"I didn't want to rush them," she says. "I wanted this to seem like a normal day." I have made sandwiches for the trip, peanut butter and jelly, and the eldest girl takes that shopping bag murmuring thanks.

We say good-bye, embrace, Crystal says she'll call. She is grateful and I don't deserve gratitude. Here is this brave woman taking eight kids to a strange city where she knows no one, and all I can think of is please don't ask me for something I can't give. Part of me fears I will see them all tomorrow, outside the West Side Market again. But several nights later she telephones from Alabama; they have arrived safely, they have somewhere to stay, and Crystal already has a job working in a cafeteria.

For a long time afterward, I was afraid when the telephone rang. I was afraid when the downstairs buzzer sounded. I was equally afraid of seeing her again, and of never seeing her again. But my center would not hold, and I knew it, and I was most terribly afraid of who I would become when I said No.

iii

IT IS 2003. A NEW SOCIAL WORKER GREETS ME AS I walk down the hall of the neurobehavioral unit of the Northeast Center for Special Care. This is the locked ward; residents here all suffer serious behavioral problems brought on by brain injury. "Poor impulse control" is the euphemism. The young woman introduces herself, and I say I am here to visit my husband. Who is your husband? she asks. I tell her.

"Well," she chirps, much too cheerily, "we'll start work on getting Rich home."

My husband was hit by a car three years ago. He sustained traumatic brain injuries. Most of the recovery in traumatic brain injury occurs during the first year. Does this person know my husband? Does she know anything?

"I think we're way past that," I say.

"Oh. For the weekend then," she says. I am not inclined to smile. She isn't well meaning, she is on automatic. One size fits all.

I don't want to bring my husband home for the weekend. This doesn't mean I don't love him, it doesn't mean I don't miss him, but I know what's possible and what isn't. Traumatic brain injury is characterized by the following symptoms: psychosis, paranoia, hallucinations, aggressive behavior, rages.

I remember how quickly my husband's tenuous grasp of reality slipped away. He was, for all intents and purposes, a madman. He stood among bloody bodies, he was unarmed in battle, desperate and terrified. The Gestapo were coming for him. The food was poisoned, the apartment wasn't ours, it was a replica, why was I trying to fool him? He was also gentle and sweet for stretches of time, but madness held sway. Twenty-four hours a day a home health aide was there; together we tried to get him to his doctors' appointments, his outpatient rehab, into clean clothes, into his shoes, out for a walk in the park. Simple tasks were uphill sledding. What would take an ordinary person five minutes took Rich hours, and we learned to start preparing him long ahead of time, but he fell into rages and we often got nowhere. There were three shifts, everybody went home after eight hours except me and Rich. We were home.

Five weeks later, Rich was admitted to the psychiatric ward of another hospital, and from there to a rehab facility on Long Island. But he got no better, and after ten months they couldn't keep him any longer. This wasn't a locked facility, and he had gotten out of the building several times, headed up the hill toward a six-lane highway. They locked the elevator, an inconvenience for everybody, but then Rich found the stairs. They were sorry, but he wasn't improving, they couldn't keep him safe, and they needed the bed.

I remember sitting in the little office with the head of the program. I liked her very much. We had grown to know each other well over the past year. "What options do we have?" I asked. She looked uncomfortable. I could look for a nursing home with a locked unit, she said, although she knew of no place offhand, or I could take him home.

Take him home?

I was terrified. What would happen to us? Where would my life go? I wouldn't be Rich's wife; I would be his jailor and my own. This was a sacrifice that made no sense, I couldn't do it.

It has taken me almost five years to accept this about myself. What kind of woman was I? What about my wedding vows? Who was I that keeping hold of my own life was more important than taking care of my husband? I kept forgetting the fact that I actually *couldn't* take care of him. My terror obscured the truth: no single person, no two people could have taken care of a man in Rich's condition. Why then did I feel so ashamed? What standard do we women hold ourselves to? After all these years I can finally say the words *I want to live my life* without feeling unnatural, selfish, cowardly.

The social worker didn't last long.

iv

THE HOUSE FEELS LONELY WHEN I FIRST GET BACK, although the dogs are barking and jumping their greetings. I feed them, put down fresh water. If Rich has washed the dishes I take them out of the rack and wash them again, his eyesight is no good. Maybe I make myself a cup of tea. When I go into the living room the dogs follow, Rosie hopping up on the cushion behind my back on the big red chair, Harry and Carolina curling up on either end of the sofa. The blue chair where Rich sat stays empty. It takes maybe half an hour for me and the dogs to fill the house again, but we do.

Guilt

A DOOR BLEW OPEN LAST SUMMER AND A CARdinal flew through and got itself trapped on my screened-in porch. I don't know how long it was there before the dogs started barking. It was a small bird, or maybe it just looked small, beating its red wings and banging against the screen opposite the door. I locked the dogs in the kitchen and went out waving my arms around, giving instructions in English. "No, you idiot bird, turn around, the door is behind you, *behind you,*" which only alarmed it further. I got a broom and tried to shoo it to freedom, but this didn't work either. I began to wonder how long it had been there, and how long before its wild heart gave out. I went back for a towel and luckily I managed to throw it over the bird on the first try. When I gathered it up I could feel the little body thrumming through the folds of terry cloth—amazing—and then I released it, and watched it fly high into the branches of a pine, a blotch of red against the green. The screen door was falling off its hinges. I shut it and propped a chair under the knob so the wind wouldn't blow it open again.

I bring up the bird because I'm interested in guilt these days.

Thirty years ago, my old friend Quin took a step back and the heel of his shoe cracked a kitten's skull. He carried the little thing into the bathroom and filled the sink with warm water and held the kitten under because it wasn't dead, wouldn't die, despite the blood leaking out of its eyes and mouth. After an endless minute he lifted it up and the tiny creature gasped for breath. So he held it under again, and then again, until all nine lives had given up the ghost. Before it was over, the water had turned pink and then red. Quin didn't talk for the rest of the afternoon.

I don't know the connection between these animals and guilt. But here's another one, a raccoon I saw on the Palisades Parkway two years ago. It must have been hit by the car ahead of me, because when I drove past, the left half of its body was smashed against the road while the right half still pawed frantically at the air. The ng would have been to hit it again, but I didn't think fast enough, and couldn't have done it. I'm stuck with the image. It doesn't fade.

I am thinking about animals, and guilt, staring at the fire, my dog Rosie sleeping on the cushion behind my back. I want to look up *guilt,* but am too lazy to find the dictionary, and outside the blizzard snow is coming down like soft white dinner plates, and I am cozy. I am obsessed by guilt because I think mine's gone, at least the all-purpose kind that makes you feel you are to blame for a bad dinner party at which you are only a guest, that toxic mist that can be activated by small offenses, or—as in when somebody's else's party never gets off the ground—no offense at all. ("Don't worry about it, they probably invited you at the last minute," says my friend Chuck.) Recently I did something thoughtless, and caused someone to do hours of work for what turned out to be nothing. I was very sorry and I said so, but the stab of guilt that used to produce a familiar feeling of worthlessness didn't appear.

Finally I'm so curious that I rouse myself and find the dictionary, which is not where it should be (I am so disorganized, I'll never keep anything straight, what's *wrong* with me, I . . .). And I look up *guilt.* There are two meanings that apply to me—the first is to be responsible for committing an offense, the next is the feeling of remorse for doing so. That other guilt—the kind that doesn't discriminate—they don't mention it, but no matter. I burned out my receptors for that nonsense.

I know what real guilt is.

MY HUSBAND WAS HURT, NOT ME. I WAS SAFE IN the apartment that night, already in my nightgown, wondering what was taking Rich so long but grateful for half an hour alone. Rich had opted for early retirement; he had been a reporter and the news wasn't news anymore and this depressed and angered him. He was home all the time now, and so was I, and neither of us could get an act together. My own problems—worries about children, a restlessness I didn't understand, raw grief over the loss of an old friend—were easy to lay at Rich's door. I was used to eight hours of solitude every day and his presence derailed me. I badgered him about volunteering, nagged him about taking a course, bullied him to start writing again, all in vain. I would have done anything to get him out of the house, although I couldn't seem to get out myself. "For better or for worse, but not for lunch," my friend Liz quoted an aunt of hers, but nothing struck me funny anymore. That Monday evening I was irritable, and after supper went into the bedroom to read. Rich washed the dishes, and took the dog out. Twenty minutes became thirty became forty. I looked out the window—surely he was coming now—but could see nothing. Where was he? Maybe Harry was taking his sweet time, maybe Rich had stopped to talk to another dog owner. Then the call came from Pedro.

It took a year to realize the severity of Rich's injuries. His body was slowly recovering, but his mind was not. His grip was strong but his balance was off, he was tottery, he shuffled, he walked with his head down. I was able to walk, run, stand. I could see out of both eyes. I could remember what I'd had for breakfast. Rich's short-term memory was shot, setting him adrift in time; the damage done his frontal lobes had smashed open his own personal Pandora's box. I pieced together details—Rich imagined himself on a battlefield, he was attacked by dogs, his children were missing—looking for connections, wanting to understand what triggered what inside his head. It was like being on a psychic scavenger hunt where at the end of the day everything would make sense. On the days I didn't visit, I called. If he was having a bad day I called all the time. It was impossible to separate my life from his.

The word *permanent* was a long time coming. Rich had suffered permanent brain damage. He was never going to live at home again, never going to drive a car, read a book, make a cup of coffee. I knew this, and I didn't believe it. But fourteen months after the accident, Sally and I moved him to a long-term care facility for people with brain injuries. The staff knew what they were doing, they had seen everything, they were kind and patient and overworked and I trusted them. After a week or two, somebody gently suggested that frequent telephone calls were not necessary. I shouldn't worry. If there was a problem, they would let me know. I took this to mean that in the nicest possible way I was being told to Get a Life.

SO THAT'S WHAT I DID. I PUT A LIFE TOGETHER with my family and friends and dogs. I learned to make use of the solitude I now had aplenty. I started writing, wanting to make something useful come from our catastrophe, and working hard, I began to be happy. Rich's paranoia began to subside. Two years after Rich was hurt, I bought a house nearer to where he lived, and was able to start bringing him home for afternoons. I made new friends, I learned to knit, I watched my dogs play with no leashes. I met other writers, and we began to get together to share our work. And then one day I asked myself a terrible question. If I could make Rich's accident never have happened, would I do it? Of course I would. Wouldn't I? And instead of yes, I hesitated. But by posing the question I had assumed the power, and by hesitating I put myself behind the wheel of the car that struck my husband.

You want to talk about guilt?

I lived with this shame a long time before I could speak of it. Finally I told my sister. "But it's not about Rich's accident," Eliza said. "You don't want to return to unhappiness. That's all." I will never forget that instant of absolute clarity. And just like that, I was free.

BUT, *LOOK AT YOU,* I STILL SAY TO MYSELF. *HOW DARE you. You built this on tragedy.*

I AM TRYING TO MAKE SENSE OF THIS. SURVIVOR'S guilt, acceptance, these were words that made me roll my eyes; surely I was too sophisticated for such clichés. I thought I *had* accepted Rich's accident, even though I kept putting myself in a place where it hadn't happened yet. Rich hadn't yet left for his walk. I could stop him at the door. I thought that not accepting meant turning my face to the wall, unable to function. So now today I look up the word *acceptance* and the definition is "to receive gladly" and that doesn't sound right. I flip to the back, and look up its earliest root, "to grasp," and discover this comes from the old English for "a thread used in weaving," and bingo, that's it. You can't keep pulling out the thread. You have to weave it in and then you have to go on weaving.

I love my husband. Every time I see him there is the moment when I can't believe it. I look at his face and think only, *How did this happen to you, I can't believe this thing happened to you.* I would make him well again if I could. I would change everything about that day if I could. I wouldn't have bought the new leash that broke. I would have walked the dog myself. I would have gone with Rich to keep him company. There are days when the thread snaps and I see him in lying in Riverside Drive, his head caved in, the street wet with blood, and I gasp. But it passes. Rich is necessary to my happiness; I love the person he is now, I love who I am when I'm with him, and I can sometimes hold these two truths in my head at once: I wish he were whole, and I love my life.

IT IS A WINTER AFTERNOON. I LOOK AT THE FIRE, the dogs sleep, and my mind turns round and round finding a place to rest. We are alive. Our conversations aren't taxing. *Good dog, good dog.* They go out, and I watch them running hard on the trail of something. There is a white cat that likes the falling-down red chicken coop and she (I think of it as a she) drives the dogs crazy. I mistook her once for a possum. Sometimes there are deer exploding out of the overgrown forsythia and they bound gracefully into the woods, the dogs in hot pursuit until they reach the little white flags that signify the underground electric fence and there they stop, on a dime. I can see the deer's white tails visible for a second before they disappear into the trees. So that's where hightailing it comes from. Yesterday I found a mole on the carpet, tiny pink snout, pink paws. I was glad it was dead and not lingering, grateful that dogs don't kid around. I scooped it up with a piece of cardboard and threw its body in the trash.

I don't know why I didn't think to touch its soft fur or feel the little weight in my hand.

I wish I had.

Edward Butterman Sleeps
at Home

MY FRIEND JO INVITES ME FOR SUPPER. "We're having beef stew and three kinds of dessert," she says cheerfully. I thank her, but Rich is in the hospital, I've been there all day, and tonight I'm just going to crash. "We'll bring you the leftovers then," she says. The next morning there is Jo at the door. She hands me a package wrapped in foil. "We ate all the stew," she says, "but here are three different desserts." Rich has a sweet tooth these days and I take Jo's desserts to the hospital. He is just finishing lunch and I hand him the little package.

"What's this?" he asks. "Beef stew?"

I love this stuff. It happens all the time. Rich knows nothing of Jo, or what she made for dinner, but since the accident he knows things he couldn't possibly know. Maybe when one part of the brain is severely injured, another part kicks in. Maybe hindbrain, the earliest brain, still in there underneath our more highly evolved layers, communicated differently, without language. If we peel those layers away, maybe we've got the family heirloom.

After all, who needs words? My dogs know more about me than I know about myself. When they look at me with that imploring "no, don't do it" expression, I realize I'm about to drive into town for a cup of coffee and the paper.

The first time involved a puppy.

My friend Denise came east after the death of her beloved dog, Gus. In the old days before his accident Rich and Denise were news junkies together; it was Denise who once gave Rich fifty pencils with the words *The Nicest Man in the World* engraved on them. The second day of her visit we were downtown shopping, and on the sidewalk in front of the store there was a woman holding a gangly cream-colored puppy. He was a white Doberman, ears and tail intact, and he was for sale. I watched Denise's face when she took him in her arms and realized this was a done deal. That night the puppy, christened Henry, ran around the apartment with my dogs, Harry and Rosie, all three of them barking. I remember thinking how Rich would have hated the chaos. The phone rang. It was a nurse from the facility where Rich was living telling me my husband wouldn't come out of his room. He was certain Dobermans were outside his door, waiting to attack him.

Rich knew nothing of the puppy in our apartment.

TODAY RICH MENTIONS THE NAME EDDIE BUTTER-man and says something about the stock market. He has talked about an Eddie before, but without the last name.

"Who is Eddie?" I asked the first time.

"Eddie is our beloved Eddie," said Rich. "Eddie is the only Eddie around."

He unwraps the desserts and breaks a chocolate brownie, offering me half. "No thanks," I say, but he sets it apart for me on a napkin anyway.

"The lounge lizard was here again," says Rich, brownie halfway to his mouth. "Maybe I should imitate him."

"Who?" I ask. "Imitate who?"

"The lounge lizard." Rich smiles, pops the brownie in his mouth, and the conversation ends.

SIX MONTHS AGO A FRIEND WAS ANGRY WITH ME and I with her. I had written about something someone said many years ago, but it was she who heard the words, not me, a fact I had completely forgotten. Her experience was precious, and she accused me of stealing her memory. Not only that, but what she remembered with grief I had somehow transmuted to gratitude, so besides stealing her memory, I also got it wrong. We argued, but there was no meeting place. For days the same questions went through my head. Is memory property? If two people remember something differently is one of them wrong? Wasn't my memory of a memory also real? There were no solid answers, just winding paths I went round and round on. I thought of nothing else; a chasm had opened between me and my friend.

When I went to see Rich that Thursday, the first thing he said was "Please forgive the selfishness of an old man who seizes the past for his own." He paused, but I was already listening closely. This sounded oddly like what I'd been thinking about. ". . . a version of the past, Eddie may not have experienced anything like it but he realized with the turn of a page that he could do storytelling . . . the first abundance of retelling fairy tales and fables and legends would come from their mouths—Eddie's and your father's."

I scrounged around in my pocketbook and found my pen and notebook.

"Once one goes to the trouble of becoming a story-teller," Rich continued, "they want the whole magilla—not only to be the first but the only—I'm not saying that occurred. I'm always glad when it does as long as feelings aren't hurt." I scribbled as fast as I could. "Eddie's fables include multiple storytellers but none of them feels at any loss if they're not the first or second out of the dugout. The art of storytelling is too various to have any one person have complete control."

He was speaking slowly, pausing as if giving dictation. I was amazed at what I was hearing. Not only did Rich know nothing of the argument, he wouldn't have been capable of understanding it. On top of that, he had never before stuck to any subject for more than a sentence or two. And here he was holding forth so eloquently on just what had been obsessing me. ". . . that method of storytelling is forgotten, that time of Eddie's in which everyone seemed to add memory on memory deep in the forest, layers of dirt and leaves and branches get covered up — in a sense the past is underfoot."

I was present at a miracle.

SO NOW WHEN RICH MENTIONS EDDIE BUTTER-man in the hospital I call his brother. "He was a cousin on our father's side," says Gil. "We never called him Edward. He was always Eddie. He did something in the stock market, married a shoe heiress, ran around a lot, everyone knew him at the racetrack. He even wore a checkered jacket like in *Guys and Dolls*. He disappeared out west years ago. Nobody knows what happened to him."

RICH IS IN THE HOSPITAL BECAUSE LAST FRIDAY HE didn't know who I was. At first I thought he was kidding, I thought I could see him laughing behind his eyes. First I shouted, then I begged — talk to me right now, this minute, talk to me. He didn't respond to anything, not me, not the nurses, not his arm being jostled, or even his shoulder shaken — usually a surefire way to raise his ire. Nothing. They took his blood pressure, fine; no temp, fine. But he wasn't there. And when he began to come back from wherever he'd been, he couldn't walk. He couldn't even stand. The word *seizure* got thrown around, the word *stroke*.

A COUPLE OF YEARS AGO, DENISE AND I WERE IN Mexico, both of us counting the days until we would be back with our dogs. We were pathetic. San Miguel was great, roosters and flowerpots on rooftops; our house was up a steep cobblestone street, the food was delicious, and all we wanted to do was get on a plane and go home to our dogs. One morning I was trying to get through to Rich on the telephone. He was at the Northeast Center for Special Care in Lake Katrine, New York, and I was in San Miguel de Allende, Mexico, hollering into the receiver, intent on making him hear me, willing him not to let the phone slide away from his ear. I was staring at a tile on the counter as I shouted, "Rich? Rich? Can you hear me?"

"Hello," he said, somewhat cautiously.

"How are you?" I shouted, my eyes still drilling into the terra-cotta square.

"Fine," he answered.

"What have you been doing?" I shouted. There was a pause.

"We made some tiles today," he said.

When I got home I checked. I even talked to the person in charge of art and recreation. Nobody had made tiles, not that week, not ever.

I HAVE ALWAYS BELIEVED (IF RATHER UNEASILY) IN the invisible world. I know people who have had messages from the dead. My sister has premonitions. Once in a while somebody sits down at the foot of my bed and I feel the mattress give and wake to no one, just an air of friendliness in the room. Sober citizens I know have seen ghosts. But Rich had no truck with any of it. He was a reporter, he needed evidence, there was none. I wonder what the old Rich would have to say about the new Rich.

———

Lunch is over, Rich has fallen asleep. "He was a heavy smoker, wasn't he?" three doctors have asked, after looking at his swollen legs. "No," I tell them, wondering what's in store for me, a sixty-three-year-old woman smoking a pack a day. "Rich never smoked," I say, and they look surprised. Well, that is not strictly true. Rich told me that all together in his life he had smoked parts of six cigarettes.

I got hypnotized once to stop smoking. I smoked three packs a day and one late night, condensing George Steinbrenner's biography for the *New York Post* (nothing negative, they told me), I finished four. I called a hypnotist the next day, although hypnotism scared me. What if I couldn't come back from wherever I went? I imagined myself dangling at the end of a fishing rod, flung far into a lake, unable to be reeled back in. What would become of me? Who would inhabit my body? The hypnotist had a long gray ponytail and love beads. "I haven't lost a patient yet," he said. I walked in a smoker and three hours later walked out with no interest in cigarettes. That lasted twenty years.

My daughter Jennifer knows I'm smoking. She can tell over the phone. "I'm just drinking tea," I tell her. She is expecting twins in August, and has every reason to want her mother healthy. "No," I say, "of course I'm not smoking. Do you think I'm crazy?"

A few months ago I was wondering about whether I could afford to hang on to my apartment in the city as well as live full-time up here in this house. Winter was coming and the price of oil high, and the roof would need replacing soon, not to mention offspring who could use help now and then. I worried about this a lot. I tried to imagine selling the place I'd lived for almost thirty years. I didn't feel a huge pang, since all my stuff is up here, what's left of my apartment looks like somebody's half-eaten sandwich. But still, but still.

On Thursday I went to pick Rich up and bring him home for the afternoon.

"I can't leave" was the first thing he said to me.

"Why not?" I asked.

"We've got to sell the apartment," he says, "the real estate lady is coming today." It had been years since Rich mentioned the apartment. I didn't think he even remembered it.

I'M VISITING RICH EVERY DAY AT THE HOSPITAL. I leave my cigarettes in the car. Stroke victims, heart attacks all up and down this floor of the hospital. Is this what I want? I don't even like smoking. I don't want a cigarette. But something with a longer reach than me wants one, and I wind up smoking a pack a day. Ridiculous.

The third day Rich tells me his foot is going to be amputated. He is calm, matter-of-fact. "No," I reassure him. "Nobody's going to amputate your foot. Your foot is fine," but then I wonder. Maybe the episode left him without feeling. Maybe he was numb. Was that why he couldn't stand? Here was a possible clue as to what happened. I stroke his foot. "Can you feel that?" He nods. "That?" he nods again.

"How much sensation makes a toe?" he asks.

NOT SO LONG AGO I WAS ASKED TO WRITE AN ESSAY about being a caregiver. *But I'm not a caregiver,* I wanted to say, *I'm a wife.* I scribbled notes for days, weeping with frustration and sadness, still defensive, still justifying my decision not to bring Rich home to live. *But I couldn't have done it,* I kept reminding myself, *nobody could have.* When I went to see Rich that week he mentioned our troubles. "What are your troubles?" I asked, and clear as a bell, this was his answer: "I want to leave this place and go back to New York City. I don't think they're doing much for me here and I think I could be released in your care."

————

I KEEP WONDERING WHERE RICH WENT WHEN HE vacated his premises. He sat on a chair in the common area, his head down, hands folded. His face was expressionless. But it's impossible not to interpret even a blank look; our species' survival can depend on our ability to read a face. Years from now I may remember Rich's empty gaze as a look of bemused affection, as if he were saying, "What is all the fuss about, leave me alone, I'm fine, I'm just sitting out back in the sun." Because that's what I want to believe.

I remember where I went. When I was hypnotized I went barefoot down a bunch of pink marble stairs, soft underfoot, and at the bottom was a grassy bank and a blue lake. I was damp clay, ready to receive. When I came back up those stairs, I was peaceful. When I left the office I walked home slowly, my face turned to the sun. When Rich returned from wherever he'd been, he was fighting mad. But maybe we yanked him from somewhere he wanted to stay. How to know?

After a week Rich is sprung from the hospital. His doctors are thorough and nice and one of them keeps sheep. They have run every kind of test and all his results are normal. Hallelujah. The consensus is that he was dehydrated and that is what caused what we now refer to as the episode, the event. Dehydrated. We are

KNITTING 2002 TO PRESENT

112 shawls

½ sweater

¼ sweater

47 hoodies

34 cowl adaptations

17 blankets

29 ponchos

52 hats

15 things with ruffles to keep you warm

323 scarves

1 dog-bed blanket

⅔ wedding blanket

34 neck cozies (my own invention)

1 headband

and white clouds. In the upper right-hand corner, a yellow sun with a smiley face. I used to stand in front of this painting before I went upstairs to see my husband and then again before I went home because it cheered me up. After a couple of weeks I got up the nerve to ask if the artwork was for sale, and if so, could I please buy the painting above the drinking fountain.

It was for sale. I couldn't believe my luck. Bill Richards, the painter who ran the art studio at the center, introduced me to the artist, Ed Kindberg, a shy man in a wheelchair. Ed had never painted before he came to the Northeast Center, and now he couldn't stop. I bought the painting from him and then I bought two more. I couldn't stop either. Ed was happy, but I was obsessed. Every time I came to see Rich I first made a beeline for the art studio. Ed's work was changing. The rooftops of his houses resembled the ears of a cat, and he began painting cats' heads floating in the sky above the houses. The hills got blacker, and Ed began painting huge crosses looming over the landscape in a dark sky. These paintings were frightening and beautiful. It wasn't enough to own a few of Ed's paintings, it was as if each piece was supposed to be mine, and when I became embarrassed at how many I was buying I bought them for my friends. Another painter at the center always drew three women—different colored pens or pencils, different faces, clothes—but always three women. I picked one, and then I realized it wasn't enough. Her work was about many versions of three women, and I wanted my experience of her art to be closer to hers. I bought half a dozen wonderful drawings.

I didn't know it right away, but a new world had just opened up. I read an article in the *New York Times* about Bill Richards and his studio at the Northeast Center, and I learned that other institutions had art programs, and that this kind of work is called Outsider Art. I found books, and began to learn a little. The term Outsider Art generally refers to self-taught artists, very often these are people who live on the margins of society, but it has its roots in the art of the insane, first noticed in Europe the late nineteenth century and then celebrated in the first half of the twentieth, by the artist Jean Dubuffet. Dubuffet named it Art Brut, raw art. He championed it as the real thing, art unpolluted by society's expectations or a culture's constrictions. This was art that came straight from the psyche without a filter. The artists were the mentally ill—men and women in insane asylums—and they used whatever medium was at hand. One man made sculpture out of chewed bread; another, Adolf Wölfli, received a pencil and two pieces of blank newsprint every Monday, and he worked obsessively until there was nothing left but the bit of lead

or the history of art except what I've learned through osmosis. But Outsider Art is its own context. I don't have to know all about the Impressionists or the Abstract Expressionists. I don't have to be able to fit this art into any historic chronology. I don't feel like an ignoramus. Irony of ironies, I don't feel like an outsider—to fall in love I only need eyes.

I began to buy more and more. From a gallery I bought a short-legged horse drawn in crayon on old shirt cardboard, the words *Jesus Wept* in the lower left-hand corner, one of four such drawings that had hung in the bedroom of a sharecropper's cabin. I loved the horse immediately, but when I found out where it had come from, everything got personal. I imagined a woman, heavy and tired. I tried to imagine the cabin she'd lived in, I wondered how big it was, and what kind of bed she'd slept in. Electricity or candles or kerosene? I saw a sagging front porch and inside a threadbare blanket hung to cordon off the bedroom, but then I remembered four drawings, and thought four walls. I wondered whether the floor was wooden or dirt, and then in the middle of conjuring nothing but poverty, I looked again at the words *Jesus Wept* written in beautiful old-fashioned script. And I realized I knew nothing.

From a man at the Northeast Center I bought words that went down the page in three columns: agonized proposals of marriage; I bought a page covered with letters of the alphabet, drawn in pencil by a man who was afraid he was going to forget how to write. Among the letters are numbers and what look like sketches of houses, and slanted lines that remind me of snow fences leaning away from an imaginary wind. I bought the message of a man who suffers from left neglect, a condition in which brain injury has rendered invisible the left side of everything. His words start in the middle of the page, and go off to the right, writing over and over until there is nothing but a black unreadable mass, the only parts still legible are the two original words: FORGIVE ME.

"LOOK AT THIS, LOOK AT THIS." I USED TO GRAB everyone who came to my apartment and take them on a tour whether they liked it or not. "This is by Sybil Gibson, she began painting when she was in her fifties and it started out as wanting to make her own wrapping paper and then she couldn't stop," or, "This is by an unemployed construction worker who was on the streets and he wandered into a church and they gave him paint and brushes and paper and he began painting and look!" Mostly I got patient smiles and blank looks. Then I went with my sister to the Outsider Art Fair, which is held every year at the Puck Building in New York City, and all around I saw people with the same crazed excited expression that was on my face. I bought a painting of black and white whales in a dark blue sea. I bought a scratching of the human form with letters streaming from its genitals. I bought a bunch of flowers that after I got it home and hung it up reminded me of two big purple toes and was shortly thereafter consigned to the closet. On the corner of Broadway and 111th Street, I bought four paintings of a spaceship hovering above the Statue of Liberty. The colors are vivid—violets, blacks, blues, yellows, reds. The way the disk is descending reminds me of the Annunciation, only in this case the angel Gabriel is a spaceship and the Virgin Mary is the Statue of Liberty. I think I remember the painter hinting that he had once been abducted, but I might have made that up.

I bought flowers painted on paper bags and buses painted on pieces of wood, and farm scenes painted on the six panes of an old window frame. I bought the terrifying scribbles of a schizophrenic. I bought art by famous outsider artists like Thornton Dial and Sybil Gibson and Justin McCarthy and Clementine Hunter. I bought anonymous art from psychiatric institutions, art from drug programs where the artist uses only his first name. I bought art off the street, from galleries, from big Outsider Art shows, from artists themselves. Over my desk I have hung the work of Southern artist J. B. Murry, an illiterate prophet who wrote in his own kind of hieroglyph—"spirit writings"—and then read aloud what he wrote by looking at the work through a glass of well water, an old African custom. From where I sit it resembles a topographical map, I see mountain ranges, lakes, rivers, each separate territory outlined in silver or black ink. I look at it all the time.

I DIDN'T START WRITING UNTIL I WAS FORTY-seven. I had always wanted to write but thought you needed a degree, or membership in a club nobody had asked me to join. I thought God had to touch you on the forehead, I thought you needed to have something specific to say, something important, and I thought you needed all that laid out from the git-go. It was a long time before I realized that you don't have to start right, you just have to start. Put pen to paper, allow yourself the freedom to write badly, to get it wrong, stop looking over your own shoulder. *You idiot,* I would say to myself after half a page. *What makes you think you can write,* and then I'd crumple it up and aim for the wastebasket. Then one day somebody told me a story about a daughter at her mother's funeral, and something in the story caught in my mind and wouldn't let go of me. I tried to write it and failed, but instead of throwing it away (*you idiot, give it up*), I tried again, from a different angle. I realized that I had been imitating the voice of the woman who told me the story, but it didn't ring true coming from me. I decided to make the funeral my own, and to imagine one of my daughters as the narrator, and after three hours I had three pages that I actually liked. I was off and running. For the first time a story was more important than my ego, and the know-it-all voice that told me not to bother held no sway.

That's the voice I need to banish every morning. I sit at my desk and stare at J. B. Murry's map, and the crayoned horse, and the red houses, and try to forget everything unnecessary—which is just about everything—so I can look around as if for the first time. Sometimes I think of it as waiting for an aquarium to settle. Hard to explain and harder to do, but I believe this much—wherever it is I have to get back to, these artists are already there.

BEFORE I MOVED UP HERE AND BEGAN BRINGING Rich home, we went to Bill's studio every week. The studio is housed in a two-story atrium with a glass ceiling, and when it got hot, Bill put up a kind of tent/awning over the long tables where people were working. When it rained you had to stop everything and marvel at the sound. I looked forward to the energy there,

I loved watching people work hard. I have never seen so much color in one place before or since. Everyone here has either brain injury or spinal cord injury resulting from accidents or strokes or degenerative diseases. There were people sitting at the long table, others working in wheelchairs, with special easels set at an angle; one man, a paraplegic, painting with a head-stick, who had painted the most beautiful green labyrinth made of running deer. Bill was everywhere at once, refilling paint trays, bringing more pencils, encouraging, taking the work so seriously that the artists did too. Bill wasn't teaching art, he was providing an atmosphere in which people could generate their own best work. Bill makes anything seem possible. It's a gift, a presence he has.

Rich did some drawing there, and sometimes he painted. The first thing was a duck—the figure he had always doodled. How about a few more? Bill suggested. Rich obliged, he drew another and another. Then his hand seemed to spring free, and began roaming the page in larger swoops and freer forms.

When Rich drew, I was excited.

"What's that?" I'd ask, looking at a lot of cross-hatching, and what looked like bridges, running figures.

"Well, that is two wizards, and those are the gulls and turtles protecting their habitat."

He drew a jaunty looking man in a straw hat, he

drew soldiers. He drew an island with two palm trees bending in the wind, and some other odd-looking vegetation. From one tree hung a big sign that reads, "Welcome home Abby and Rich," then in the air next to it, "Welcome home you two globe-trotters." I love this drawing. Except it breaks my heart.

One afternoon Rich was drawing what looked to be a figure lying in the middle of a circle of tiny skyscrapers. I thought about the accident, his body lying in the street.

"What are you drawing?" I asked, heart in mouth.

"A clock," he said, and he drew another one, with numbers. Later he told me he'd spoken with his mother that morning. "I don't know what she makes of it all," he said.

"What all?" I asked, not reminding him his mother died years ago. Maybe he had spoken with her. I no longer know anything for sure.

"You live with a man for sixty-two years and then one day he doesn't appear. *Oh well.* Is that what you say?" Then he sighed.

But I had no answer for that.

RICH DIDN'T ALWAYS WANT TO GO TO THE STUDIO, and once there he didn't always want to draw. We put clean paper and pencils and markers in front of him, sometimes he picked them up and sometimes he didn't. Once in a while, to get him started, I'd pick up a crayon or a Magic Marker but my attempts even to doodle were embarrassingly stiff. I was an imposter. I'm comfortable with words, it secures me to have a pen and notebook even if all I'm writing is *butter sugar milk eggs*. I looked around the studio, sopping up some of the energy in that room to take home with me. One afternoon I sat across the table from a young woman with short brown hair. She stared at a blank piece of paper, in front of her a box of freshly sharpened colored pencils. "What do you want to draw?" I asked. She didn't answer. I asked again and waited. "A face," she said finally, but she made no move. "Why don't you start with the eyes then?" I suggested. She chose a reddish brown pencil from the box and carefully drew a wavery brown line. She looked up. The nose, I suggested, another wavery line. The mouth. Soon there were a number of trembling lines on the page. You might not have known it was a face, but you knew something was going on, it hummed.

THERE WAS A YOUNG MAN WHO HAD ARRIVED AT the Northeast Center angry and belligerent, as inclined to take a swing at you as not. He began showing up in Bill's studio and started to paint. Bill watched him

Running

EVERY DAY I EXCHANGE MONEY FOR GOODS. I put bills and coins into the hand of the cashier and gather my milk and bread. Sometimes I say no thank you, no bag, and stuff orange juice into my pocketbook. In one store I get a 10 percent discount for being sixty-three or older. That's where I buy my expensive olive oil. I go to Liberty House and greet my friends (it's difficult to shop because we are always catching up) but finally I choose some interesting large garments, push plastic across the counter, sign the curly piece of paper, and walk out with a shopping bag full of possibility. ("Shopping is hope, Mom"—my daughter's words have become my mantra.) Sometimes I choose a new lipstick and different shampoo or I stare for ten minutes at all that interesting toothpaste. Later I drive to the hideous mall with a view of mountains and go shopping for shoes for my husband. He wears size 12W. "You have to go to the men's department for those," says the saleswoman, horrified, and I wonder if she is trying not to look down at my feet.

"These are our best sellers," says a young man, pointing proudly to a table full of New Balance sneakers. I suppose we don't call them sneakers anymore but I'm too old to bother with new concepts. "They are good for everything—jogging or running or walking," he says helpfully. My husband will shuffle in these shoes. But that's better than nothing. They will look familiar and comfort him and he will think he has just returned from a run or is planning one later in the day. When I get home I take them out of the box and breathe in their funny chemical smell. "Nothing like a new pair of running shoes," Rich used to say, lacing up. I allow myself a quick memory of Rich getting ready, bending stiffly from the waist for his warm-ups. When he came home he smelled like vinegar.

Or I buy a cappuccino and five chocolate chip cookies at Bread Alone and try not to bite into one if it's Thursday because I'll eat them all up in the car and they are for Rich, chocolate chips being his favorite. Or I sit in my red chair and contemplate venetian blinds for all my living room windows and wonder if I should get skinny or wide slats. If I act now I can save $150 on installation. But I don't act now. I take a nap and then I go out and buy chicken thighs and anchovies and red wine. I buy lavender soap. I buy wool and different colored potato chips.

Rich was a runner. He ran for the joy of it. He ran to clear his head. After he retired, running gave a rhythm to his days. Get up; drink coffee; eat cornflakes; read the paper; digest; get into running clothes (ancient T-shirt, spiffy new shorts), stretch (cursory), remark on the fitness of weather for a run; run; drink Gatorade and eat doughnut; rinse running clothes in sink; take shower; hang running clothes over shower rod; discuss quality of run with wife; drink more Gatorade; write in log; lie down for an hour, spent and happy.

Running organized him.

Rich organizes me. Thursday is the fixed point in my week. I get up, drink coffee, avoid the paper, vacuum rugs so his granddaughter, Nora, won't find the awful things that drop off dogs. Bake dessert or stick chicken in oven depending on weather and mood. Tidy the kitchen, close the door to my bedroom if there is laundry on the floor, round up dogs, if outside put inside. Drive to Northeast Center for Special Care. Try to find parking space close to the front so Rich won't have too far to walk. Sign in at desk in lobby, accept the sticker that says "Family" and fix it to my bag. Walk past a drawing of house with the words "I plan to move to PO Box 1325 in Glendale," go back and read again.

I TAKE THE HUGE ELEVATOR TO THE SECOND FLOOR and look around for Rich. He used to walk all the time but recently his gait is clumpy and uneven and he has difficulty getting to his feet. I go down the corridor, take a deep breath before knocking and pushing open his door. There he is, sitting in his chair, newspaper in his lap. I experience simultaneous feelings of joy and dismay. I have a sudden vision of life without Rich. It would not be like falling through space without a safety net, it would be like falling through space with a parachute but no planet to land on.

I bought myself a pair of costly running shoes long ago and for a brief period (two days) Rich and I ran together—or rather I attempted to run and he jogged at my side—and I made it about two blocks before collapsing. It was fun. I forget why we stopped, maybe it got too hot. Rich kept a running log for thirty years. His entries included the weather, time of day, where and how far he ran. If he felt strong he said so, if he weakened he made note of when. Rarely did other details make it into his book—this wasn't a diary, but on April 8, 1988, after the weather and other physical facts he wrote: tomorrow—marry Abby.

The Past, Present, Future

"HOW'S YOUR LOVE LIFE?" SOMEONE ASKED me last winter. I hadn't seen this person since the eighth grade. We went to *Love Me Tender* the day it opened in 1956; it was sort of a date and I think his mother drove us. When the lights dimmed he leaned over and said, "This is probably when I should begin whispering sweet nothings in your ear." I had never heard the phrase "sweet nothings" and it charmed the hell out of me. Twenty minutes later Elvis appeared as a dot in a field and the whole audience began screaming.

"How's your love life?" I suppose it was a fair question.

"I'm married," I answered, not adding "buster," because I don't think that's what he meant.

Whatever he did mean, he didn't pursue it, but the subject was raised and I had to think it over. Did he assume I was lonely? Did he think I ought to be out in the world, prowling around for another partner? Even if I wanted to—and I don't—I couldn't face all the talking. The past is not as interesting to me now as it was when I was young, and it would certainly come up. There's nothing I want to relive—certainly not youth—and as for what's to come, I'm in no hurry. I watch my dogs. They throw themselves into everything they do; even their sleeping is wholehearted. They aren't waiting for a better tomorrow, or looking back at their glory days. Following their example, I'm trying to stick to the present. I'm not stranded here, I know where I've been; I can conjure up details of old haunts, even former states of mind.

ALTHOUGH THE FUTURE IS GOBBLING UP MY OLD city neighborhood. Where once there was sky on all four corners, there is a large charmless apartment building and across the street—we are talking about Broadway and 110th—there is a big hole where another new apartment building is going up. Gone is the West Side Market, Columbia Bagel, Dynasty Restaurant. Gone is the Ideal Bookstore and the little place that sent packages by UPS. I can still remember when we had three fruit and vegetable stands spilling onto the sidewalk within two blocks of each other. Now there is a hermetically sealed Gristede's (why does all that indoor fruit look so shiny?) and nowhere is the eye drawn to an outdoor blaze of color, all of it edible.

I spent some of my salad days in the West Side Market, and the long-gone Cathedral Market, I flirted with butchers and cheese mongers and the produce manager. I was in my prime moving among the oranges and eggplants and celeries and apples and artichokes in their boxes and pyramids on the street. I had an admirer, a older gentleman who wore a sombrero and a black string tie. He was a tall man, and often drank from something in a brown paper bag, and he murmured "pretty lady" when we passed each other on the sidewalk. On days I wasn't looking my best I'd cross the street lest he have to pretend, saying "pretty lady" when it was really sad lady or tired lady or no lady at all. He was gallant. It's easy now—it's middle-aged lady, nobody's looking, nobody notices. I go without lipstick if I feel like it, and I always wear my comfy clothes. It's a life with fewer distractions, but should something beautiful show up, a middle-aged woman is free to stare.

There was a husband and wife who used to have a drugstore on the west side of Broadway between 110th and 111th. It was a small, old-fashioned place, and we always shopped there instead of the discount chain that had opened across the street. The owners were Eastern

Europeans, and their forearms bore tattoos. Every evening they strolled out together, the woman's cheeks rosy, her silver hair held in place by beautiful combs. My memory puts them arm in arm. They were a shy, courteous couple, the husband bowing slightly if our eyes met, his wife smiling in recognition, nodding her head. They walked an old dog. The drugstore has been gone probably twenty-five years, I can't remember what replaced it or even what part of the block it occupied, but theirs was the kind of marriage I wanted, so comfortable you probably didn't even have to talk.

Rich and I don't make conversation; we exchange tidbits, how well we've slept, what was for breakfast. We are stripped down to our most basic selves, no static, no irony, no nuance. Once in a while Rich says something that takes my breath away: "I feel like a tent that wants to be a kite, tugging at my stakes," he said one day, out of a clear blue sky. He was lying in a hospital bed, but his eyes were joyous. In some ways we are simply an old married couple, catapulted into the wordless phase ahead of time. An old pal of mine used to extol the virtues of basic body warmth in the days when I was more into the heat, but now I understand. Rich and I sit together, we hold hands; we are warm-blooded creatures in a quiet space, and that's all the communication we need.

But I have to resist the impulse to create memories suitable for framing. I have to resist the impulse to preserve us at our most content. Rich is restless. Some days he can't sit still. He is unsteady, and needs help getting to his feet. We walk through the house together. Do you want a cup of coffee? water? the bathroom? No, no, and no. Rich just needs to be moving. And I ask myself what use is a destination anyway?

RECENTLY SOMEONE ASKED ABOUT MY WORST fears—what were they? I couldn't come up with anything. To have a fear you have to be able to imagine the future, and I never think about the future anymore. It is no longer my destination. There are lots of things I don't want to have happen, of course. I don't want to have a flat tire or get lost driving at night or be eaten by wild animals. I don't want to lose my mind or my livelihood. I don't want to forget where I parked the car or the names of my children but I'll jump off that bridge when I come to it, as an old friend used to say. I did recently Google "fluid in the inner ear" and worried briefly about obscure ways to go deaf, because my left ear was clicking, but that went away—the fear and the clicking—after a Sushi Deluxe with Claudette at the Wok and Roll in Woodstock. But as for fears, I don't have any.

You do so, says my sister Judy.

I do not, I say.

Then why can't you get in my elevator?

That's a phobia, I tell her.

Phobia means fear! she says. Don't you know any Greek?

MAYBE IT'S ALL SEMANTICS. MY DEFINITION OF fear is that it's a constant companion, a sidekick, riding you like a watch, going in and out of the days. I don't live like that anymore. The fact that I'm sixty-three has something to do with it. What I used to fear was growing old—not the aches and pains part or the what-have-I-done-with-my-life part or the threat of illness, none of that. I just couldn't imagine what my life would be like without the option of looking good.

I had a piece of good luck. I married Rich in my late forties and thus was eased into middle age while living with a man who approved of the way I looked. When after three years of marriage I lamented the fact that I had put on a good deal of weight, he said, "Don't worry. I love it all. You can get as fat as you want." Then, upon reflection, he added sweetly, "As long as you can still get up from your chair."

———

WHEN RICH AND I FIRST MET, WE WANTED TO know every last thing about each other. The past was still damp and new, full of clues—it was the way to make sense and order of our lives, and to illustrate who we had become. Rich listened to stories of my marriages and my parents and my sisters and my kids, and I listened to his. We took each other's side in ancient disputes. Now, as my brother-in-law is fond of remarking, the past is in the wastebasket.

Besides, I'm okay alone. I don't always want to answer a question about why I'm coughing if I'm coughing. I like falling into *Return to a Place Lit by a Glass of Milk* without being asked what am I reading. I appreciate not being interrupted in the middle of thinking about nothing. Nobody shoos my dogs off the sofa or objects to the three of them with sardine breath farting under the covers in bed at night. I like moving furniture around without anyone wishing I wouldn't or not noticing that I have. I like cooking or not, making the bed or not, weeding or not. Watching movies until three A.M. and no one the wiser. Watching movies on a spring day and no one the wiser. To say nothing of the naps.

Getting back to the question. How is my love life? Rich is my husband. We have been married seventeen years. We fall asleep together on the couch, trusting and comfortable and warm. That's my love life, it's all I want and I can have it anytime. All I have to do is drive to the Northeast Center, pick up my husband, and drive him home. But what with one thing and another—my icy driveway, big snowstorms, various colds—there were two months this winter when I couldn't. I chickened out every week, afraid I wasn't strong enough to help him with the steps, afraid of us both slipping and falling in the snow. When I was younger I never fell, and if I did, so what? Now I am brittle-boned, full of aches and pains, and I watch my step. Being cautious is new territory; my specialty was leaping, not looking. These days I pay attention. You can stumble uphill as easily as down. Ice comes in smooth and corrugated. Plastic bags are slippery underfoot. A big dog can knock you to your knees.

WHEN WE STAY AT THE NORTHEAST CENTER, we hang out in the room. He sits in the chair with his part of the paper, and I sit on his bed with mine. When I glance over, his head is bowed, the paper on his lap. There are a couple of pictures of flowers on the wall, some photos of Sally and the baby, there is a green-checked quilt on the bed. Two bird calendars hang off tacks, one showing March, the other May. There is a corn plant, a spider plant; Sally bought him beautiful deep blue hydrangeas. But if Rich falls asleep, all I see is what my husband looks like alone.

THE FIRST DECENT DAY I COULD, I BROUGHT RICH back to the house. It had rained and flooded and rained again, and the ice was finally almost gone, replaced by mud. Rich was silent on the drive, not remarking on the usual landmarks, nor did he appear to recognize the house. It felt like ages to me since he'd been here, but I don't know how it felt to Rich. I don't know how he absorbs time. I like it better when I bring him home. We have a busy routine — cups of tea, lunch, more tea, cookies, doing dishes. In good weather, we'll take a walk, or sit outside. If Rich needs his nails clipped, Sally does it. If he needs a haircut, Sally does it. She is careful and patient. Last week he needed a haircut. Yes, he wanted one, but not now. Rich was stubborn before the accident, he is ten times more stubborn since. All the "it will only take a minute"s were to no avail. He wouldn't budge. "Not now," he said for the third time, an edge in his voice. We all stood ankle deep in that long moment, and then he sat down in the chair, Sally put the towel around his shoulders and went to work.

Five minutes into the haircut, Rich dozed off. Nora was carefully eating Cheerios, the dogs were behaving themselves for a change. Sally combed and cut, combed and cut. Rich looked peaceful. There is a volunteer barber at the Northeast Center, but Rich walks past without stopping. He is always walking, the nurses tell me; when he is poorly, he holds the railing along the walls of the corridors. Last week I found him in the corridor nearing the elevators. He told me he was looking for "the door to," "the place where," and then he gave up, unable to finish.

After the haircut, Rich wanted to go upstairs. The stairs worry me and I've always talked him out of the second floor. Most of the time he doesn't even notice that there are stairs. Suppose he lost his balance and I lost mine? I don't have strength enough to keep him safe, I can't even lift his old typewriter anymore. "But why do you want to do that?" I asked him. "There's nothing interesting upstairs." By then I'd steered him into the living room and we were sitting together on the sofa. The fire was lit, the dogs were snoring away.

"I should put my combs and brushes in their new places," he said happily.

WHEN I WAS YOUNG, THE FUTURE WAS WHERE ALL the good stuff was kept, the party clothes, the pretty china, the family silver, the grown-up jobs. The future was a land of its own, and we couldn't wait to get there. Not that youth wasn't great, but it came with disadvantages; I remember the feeling I was missing something really good that was going on somewhere else, somewhere I wasn't. I remember feeling life passing me by. I remember impatience. I don't feel that way now. If something interesting is going on somewhere else, good, thank god, I hope nobody calls me. Sometimes it's all I can do to brush my teeth, toothpaste is just too stimulating.

The future was also the place where the bad stuff waited in ambush. My children were embarking on their futures in fragile vessels, and I trembled. I wanted to remove obstacles, smooth their way, I wanted to change their childhoods. I needed to be right all the time, I wanted them to listen to me, learn from my mistakes, and save themselves a lot of grief. Well, now I know I can control my tongue, my temper, and my appetites, but that's it. I have no effect on weather, traffic, or luck. I can't make good things happen. I can't keep anybody safe. I can't influence the future and I can't fix up the past.

What a relief.

I WAS ON A SMALL ISLAND ONCE, IN THE MIDDLE OF a great big lake, mountains all over the place, and as I watched the floating dock the wind kicked up, the waves rose from nowhere, and I imagined myself lying there and the dock suddenly breaking loose, carried away by the storm. I wondered if I could lie still and enjoy the sensation of rocking, after all I wouldn't be dead yet, I wouldn't be drowning, just carried off somewhere that wasn't part of my plan. The very thought of it gave me the shivers. Still, how great to be enjoying the ride, however uncertain the outcome. I'd like that. It's what we're all doing anyway, we just don't know it.

Moving

i

I'M SITTING IN THE ESSAY AISLE OF BARNES &
Noble trying to change my socks. I don't have an
apartment anymore so this is my pit stop, Broadway and 83rd. On one side of me is Vivian Gornick's
Approaching Eye Level and on the other the complete es-
says of Montaigne. I'm planning to take a look at both,
but first things first. I bought new shoes on my way to
the city and wore them out of the store and the shoes
are green with pink dots and my socks don't match.
Normally this wouldn't bother me but it offends the
eyes to look at my feet. A young couple appears and
settles down at the tail end of fiction, four feet away.
They are making a sound that if they were older would
be called chuckling and he wants her to buy a book
called Sex Something-Something but she doesn't want

that one. He won't let go of her or stop doing to her whatever it is he's doing until she agrees to buy the book with sex in the title, but she continues to resist.

If I weren't busy, I'd be eavesdropping properly, but instead I'm struggling to remove the black sock with red peppers from my left foot. I had hoped for privacy. It's hard to sit on the floor and change your socks without looking as though you're sitting on the floor changing your socks, especially when you're sixty-three. I finally manage to yank them both off and slip on the new pink anklets, then slide back into my shoes. My feet are a vision of loveliness. The young couple is whispering, perhaps discussing the likelihood of my being nuts, but I don't glance in their direction. I open the Montaigne at random. "Of Drunkenesse," ah yes. You can do most anything in this friendly Barnes & Noble, as this is the branch where somebody sat undisturbed in a chair all day and all night and then at closing it turned out he was dead.

Hours later I'm sitting on a bench in front of the bagel store on Sixth Avenue and 13th eating an everything bagel with cream cheese and trying not to spill any of it on my student's story when a gentleman with reddish gray stubble on his face sits down next to me. This is a small bench. He smells of unwashed hair, old sweat, and he is talking. At first I think he has a cell phone because he speaks and pauses, speaks again, asking someone if he'd like to come home. I check quickly, no cell phone. He asks again, politely giving himself time to think about his answer. From the corner of my eye I see him pull a pack of cigarettes out of his breast pocket and then he searches for a light in the pocket of his jacket, which is right next to the pocket of my jacket. "Some other time," he is saying. I am still carefully eating my bagel but the everythings are falling on the title page. Finally he stands up to retrieve the matches, lights his cigarette, and sits down. Two drags later he gets up again. "Well," he says to himself, "see you tomorrow," and then he takes off.

Bagel eaten, I rummage through my bag, which is stuffed to overflowing with twenty or thirty single-spaced typed pages held together with a bobby pin and many creased, soiled manila envelopes, a camisole (I can explain everything), a pair of dirty socks, three lipsticks, one mascara wand, a paper bag stuffed with tissue paper, napkins, two empty plastic bags, one poetry anthology (paid for), three diaries full of scribblings and shopping lists, various other pieces of balled-up paper, a pen from a Realtor in a different state and another from a hotel in South Carolina, and some cutlery just in case. I have a friend who always carries a copy of the United States Constitution in her bag in case she gets a chance to read it someday. It isn't lost on me that to the casual observer I might appear for the second time today to be a person whose eye it is advisable to avoid, but I want to see if there are poppy seeds stuck in my teeth and I'm looking for my mirror. Pawing through this rubbish I'm about one plastic spoon shy of starting to shriek or mutter, but here comes my student. Well, I just won't smile at him, that's all. Thank god I changed my socks.

After class, at ten forty-five I take the subway to 111th where I parked under a construction scaffold this morning thinking *que sera sera,* and after I buy my big black coffee I am happy to find the car unscathed. This is my old neighborhood. One block from here, a painting that used to hang in my apartment went for sale on a card table in front of Academy Hardware. I know because the painter herself found it on the street and bought it back and then she called me up. I had not meant to throw it out, I told her, but in truth, I had.

I threw out everything when I moved. Thirty years of diaries. I even tossed the one that began "Today I married my darling" (but not before sitting down on the floor to read it through). It was terribly personal and terribly boring, not even useful as CliffsNotes. How liberating! The minute I threw it into the trash I remembered how the judge had been late, and the party in full swing, and I'd been afraid he wasn't coming, that he'd forgotten, or lost the address, or the phone number, that he was sick or stuck, that he was going to be a no-show. Rich put his arms around me. "Never mind," he said, "we'll go on our honeymoon and get married when we come back." Was I comforted? I must have thought that's sweet but where's the judge. Now I think, oh my god, what a nice man I married.

I drive back to Woodstock drinking coffee and blasting Leon Russell and I get home at twelve thirty to three excited dogs—there is a varmint in the yard and they'd like to get busy. Forget about it, I say, this is bear season. I breathe the night, go to bed with the rest of my pack, and wake up in the morning with a sawed-off past and a future I can't imagine.

ii

IN THE MORNING I DECIDE TO GO THROUGH THE rubbish in my bag. I gave up the keys to my old apartment, but there are still four keys left on my key ring; I have no idea what they used to unlock. I ought to throw them out too, but I'm going to hang on to them. One of them might have opened my parents' house, which was sold years ago. My sister has dreams that our parents appear at her door, asking why they can't go home. "What do you tell them?" I ask, horrified.

"I skirt the issue," she says, and we both laugh. "But there was this one dream, I think they were younger. They were in the driveway and so was I. They wanted to go in the house and I told them they'd been gone a long time and somebody else lived there now."

"Then what?" I ask.

"I don't remember," my sister says.

"How did they look? What did they say?"

"It was a dream. I woke up."

"But—"

"It was a dream," my sister says again.

THERE WAS A VERY OLD MAGNOLIA IN THEIR YARD, and I remember standing under it with my father one day when the thick petals were mostly on the ground, making a lush slippery carpet underfoot. "This is an example of nature's profligacy," my father said, rather proudly, as if he were responsible for such wild abandon. My memory has filed this together with something else he said another time—how nature wastes nothing, everything is used again and again, nothing vanishes, it only changes form. Did he say the next thing outright or did I make it up? Why go to all that trouble just to waste a soul?

V

Five Years

ONE AFTERNOON IN MARCH, IN THE middle of what Rich always called a "lie-down," I feel a hot coin in my chest, burning through my body to the bed. It goes away when I get up but then it happens again and next I think I'm feeling pains shooting down my left arm and finally I call the doctor, which is most unlike me, and she makes me come in even when I try to cancel. How are you feeling? she asks, and I tell her, well, I'm tired all the time and I sleep all the time and I can't stand to think and so I fill my life with sleep and movies and I have this burning hot coin in my chest and I can't breathe properly. Describe your day, she says, and I do, which doesn't take long. I tell her I stopped smoking to cheer her up. Well, that's good, she says, why did you do that? I tell her my husband was in the hospital and somehow I decided to quit. How is your husband? she asks. "It's been almost five years," I say, and I start to cry and can't stop. Five years sounds so permanent.

I ARRIVE AT THE NORTHEAST CENTER. RICH LOOKS good. "How are you?" I yell into Rich's ear. He smiles at me. In twenty-nine days it will be five years.

"Either I feel weak and can't find something or I feel good, inexplicably good." I love it when he talks, when he answers with more than just a word or two.

"That's great," I say, "how did you sleep?" I no longer feel silly shouting such simple questions. They are easy to hear, easy to answer.

"I don't have any trouble sleeping," says Rich. "I just replay everything."

"What do you replay?" This is curious, something new.

"The accident," he says, "with none of the ghastly details."

"What do you remember?" I'm shocked.

"I don't remember being out with the dog."

I don't remember Rich ever talking about the accident.

"What made you think of it?" I'm careful to shout and enunciate at the same time.

"Lying here." Lying here alone, I think.

"Tell me more," I say, feeling my heart pound.

"I wish I could. I wish there were more to tell."

"What else do you remember?" To keep this conversation alive, I can't allow silence.

"I don't remember anything from before. Just that I'm trying to piece together the past, the very recent past."

"What pieces do you have?" He looks calm. I don't feel calm at all.

"Just the aftermath. I don't remember anything about the dog, about running after the dog, the whole thing escapes me."

"But you're remembering it now."

"I've been remembering that aspect ever since I can remember."

"What else?" I have to keep the balloon in the air. If it touches the ground, the conversation will be over.

"Nothing else really. I don't even remember that it was raining because I would have suggested we skip the rain because it was very hilly."

We sound like two people having a normal conversation.

"You can ask me questions and I can answer them," I tell him. Rich doesn't say anything so I continue. It is suddenly terribly important that he know this: "I was upstairs when it happened. Pedro called and I ran to where you were."

"You gave out a scream?"

"I did. Many screams."

We both fall silent. I realize that what he wants to remember I am trying to forget.

A minute goes by. I ask Rich if he knows how long we've been married.

"About a year," he answers.

I shake my head. "Seventeen years," I say, "we got married in 1988 and it's 2005."

"Abby," he says, smiling, "our life has been so easy that the days glide by."